TREASURY OF LITERATURE

PRACTICE BOOK
TEACHER'S EDITION

VOICES AND REFLECTIONS

HARCOURT BRACE & COMPANY

Orlando   Atlanta   Austin   Boston   San Francisco   Chicago   Dallas   New York
Toronto   London

C O N T E N T S

UNIT 1

The Dog on the Roof / 1–5
The Speckled Band / 6–11
The Great Peanut Puzzle / 12–17
The Great Shut-Eye Mystery / 18–23
M.C. Higgins, the Great / 24–29
A Retrieved Reformation / 30–35

UNIT 2

Mother and Daughter / 36–40
A Mother in Mannville / 41–47
The Great Ancestor Hunt / 48–51
Report from Part One / 52–57
What Are You Going to Be When You Grow
      Up? / 58–62

UNIT 3

The Search for Early Americans / 63–69
Touchmark / 70–75
James Forten / 76–79
We Hold These Truths / 80–85
1787 / 86–90

UNIT 4

Great-Grandfather Dragon's Tale / 91–94
A Fall from the Sky / 95–99
The Force of Luck / 100–103
The Hero and the Crown / 104–109

UNIT 5

The Talking Earth / 110–113
Superislands / 114–117
What the Twister Did / 118–123
Men from Earth / 124–129

UNIT 6

Listen for the Singing / 130–135
Little by Little / 136–139
The Bracelet / 140–143
From Life to Poetry / 144–148
Dogsong / 149–152
Woodsong / 153–157

Skills and Strategies Index / 158

Requests for permission to make copies of any part of the work should be mailed to: Permissions Department, Harcourt Brace & Company, 6277 Sea Harbor Drive, Orlando, Florida 32887-6777.

For permission to reprint copyrighted material, grateful acknowledgment is made to the following sources:

Bradbury Press, an Affiliate of Macmillan, Inc.: From *Dogsong* by Gary Paulsen. Text copyright © 1985 by Gary Paulsen.

Harcourt Brace & Company: From "Arithmetic" in *The Complete Poems of Carl Sandburg,* Revised and Expanded Edition, by Carl Sandburg. Text copyright 1950 by Carl Sandburg, renewed 1978 by Margaret Sandburg, Helga Sandburg Crile, and Janet Sandburg. Pronunciation Key from *HBJ School Dictionary,* Third Edition. Text copyright © 1990 by Harcourt Brace & Company.

Alfred A. Knopf, Inc.: "Winter Moon" from *Selected Poems* by Langston Hughes. Text copyright 1926 by Alfred A. Knopf, Inc., renewed 1954 by Langston Hughes.

Princeton University Press: "The Lightning Flashes!" a haiku by Basho, translated by Earl Minor, from *The Encyclopedia of Poetry and Poetics,* edited by Alex Preminger et al.

Printed in the United States of America

ISBN 0-15-304990-1

1 2 3 4 5 6 7 8 9 10   030   97   96   95   94

THE DOG ON THE ROOF

Name _____

Complete the story by writing a word from the box on each line. Then write each word on the line next to its meaning.

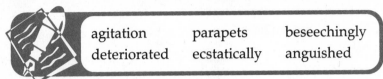

agitation	parapets	beseechingly
deteriorated	ecstatically	anguished

One afternoon when I was reading on the roof deck, I heard my dog, Spike, barking. I couldn't see him, though, even when I leaned over our rooftop __**parapets**__ to look below. When I went downstairs, Spike met me at the door, whimpering in __**agitation**__. He moved back and forth between me and the cellar door and peered up at me __**beseechingly**__. "What's up, Spike?" I asked. "Hungry?" I set down some food, but he ignored it. Although his behavior was already out of the ordinary, it soon __**deteriorated**__ even further, with more crying, scratching at the cellar door, and whining. Suddenly, he gave a loud, __**anguished**__ cry and began to bite at the doorknob. "Oh, all right," I said and pulled open the door. There sat a confused and filthy little puppy. Spike picked it up and brought it over to his supper dish, where he began licking it __**ecstatically**__. Spike will make a perfect big brother.

1. __**parapets**__ low walls on a roof

2. __**agitation**__ disturbed and troubled state

3. __**ecstatically**__ joyfully

4. __**anguished**__ distressed, full of pain

5. __**deteriorated**__ became worse

6. __**beseechingly**__ in a begging or pleading manner

THE DOG ON THE ROOF

Name _____

Fill in the prediction chart to summarize "The Dog on the Roof." **Accept reasonable responses. Possible answers are provided.**

	PREDICTIONS	WHAT ACTUALLY HAPPENS
Reasons for Living in the Park	like space and trees can't pay rent	waiting for scoundrels to pay
Reasons for Leaving the Park	police order found new place	recover money earn reward
Characters Who Help Solve Problems	Responses will vary.	Bayer Paul
Lucky Coincidences	Responses will vary.	found spinach found money

••• THE DOG ON THE ROOF •••

Name _____

Read the passage, and answer the questions.

When Mrs. Rousch opened her cottage door that blustery day in March, she had no idea of the events that would transpire in the next twenty-four hours. Secure, so she thought, on her island in the St. Lawrence River, Mrs. Rousch did not have much imagination. This trait may be why she found it hard to believe that anything would happen on the island that day.

She snorted as she watched her neighbor, Mr. Leamus, limping across the rocky bluff from his home to hers. Now *he* had an imagination, poor fool. And his cat, Blacktail, who went everywhere with him, was just as bad. Mr. Leamus actually believed Blacktail could talk with him, and he often recounted to Mrs. Rousch outlandish stories that he claimed his cat had told him. Blacktail, aloof and watchful, had never talked to Mrs. Rousch, but then she would not have believed it if he had.

1. Who are the characters in this story?
Mrs. Rousch, Mr. Leamus, Blacktail the cat _____

2. What is the setting?
an island in the St. Lawrence River, on a blustery March day _____

3. From what you have read so far, what is the plot likely to concern?
Something strange that will affect these characters is going to happen on the

island in the next twenty-four hours. _____

4. What might be the theme of the story?
Accept reasonable responses: It might concern the importance of having or

not having an imagination. _____

5. What is the mood of the passage?
expectant, suspenseful _____

6. What is the tone of the passage?
faintly mocking, pointing out Mrs. Rousch's lack of imagination _____

THE DOG ON THE ROOF

Name _____

Read the passages on these two pages, and answer the questions.
Accept reasonable responses. Possible answers are provided.

AN UNEXPLAINED DEATH

When Jared Plimpton brought his horse-drawn cab up to the darkened mansion, he had no idea what would occur during what seemed to be an ordinary evening. And it had been an ordinary evening so far. He had had several fares and was grateful for some large tips he had received. His daughter was ill, and he and his wife wanted to take her to a specialist. Every extra penny helped.

Jared yawned as he drew his horse to a stop before the ugly mansion. Rich people don't have any better taste than anyone else for all their money, he grumbled to himself. Suddenly a low moan sounded from a first-floor window. The library? Jared wondered. Or a sitting room? Then a terrifying shriek filled the night air, and Jared had to spend several seconds quieting his frightened horse.

1. What kind of story do you predict this selection will be? Why?

I predict it will be a murder mystery or a historical mystery of some kind.

The title suggests a murder. The horse-drawn cab and the ugly mansion

suggest a historical element. The mood and the setting suggest a mystery.

2. What in your previous reading experience helped you answer the first question?

Students should refer to various elements of a mystery, such as an ordinary

character in an ordinary setting who is suddenly caught up in a shocking

event.

3. Will Jared Plimpton play a major role in the mystery? Explain your answer.

Some students may suggest that since the reader learns so much about

Plimpton, he may play an important role. Others may suggest that he could

simply be part of the setting.

• • • THE DOG ON THE ROOF • • •

Name _____

BAROMETER FALLING

Cora jumped up and down and rubbed her hands together. She wished she had thought to wear her gloves and to check the bus schedule. Usually it didn't bother her to wait for the bus. She liked to bird-watch and smell the sea air coming across the dunes. But the birds were silent today, as if they were awaiting something. And Cora believed she would be nothing but a frozen statue if the bus didn't get there soon.

1. Where does this story take place?

somewhere along a seacoast

2. What kind of story do you predict it will be? Why?

Students should predict realistic fiction. The character is impatient as she

waits for a bus, a realistic reaction to an ordinary problem.

3. Do you know where the character is going on the bus? If not, tell where you *think* she is going.

I cannot tell from the information given, but I predict she is either going to

school or to town.

4. What kinds of predictions can you make about the plot?

Students should predict the plot will be about a storm or other major

weather event. The title suggests changing weather. It is obviously very

cold—colder than Cora expected, because she hasn't worn her gloves. Also,

the birds are silent, the way animals often are before a storm. The plot will

probably concern a blizzard or a cold sea storm.

• • • THE SPECKLED BAND • • •

Name _____

Read the following paragraphs. Use clues in the story to determine the meaning of each underlined word. Then write each word on the line next to its meaning.

My sister Andrea has the singular belief that she is the best detective in the country. I think she gets this attitude from my grandfather, who was a police detective. When he died, he bequeathed to Andrea his magnifying glass and fingerprint kit. He also called her his "bright granddaughter," and this allusion to her intelligence went straight to her head. Soon after, Andrea asked us for cash donations to help defray the cost of new detective equipment. Any hopes she had of collecting from my brother were soon dispelled. "I'll make a donation when we land an astronaut on Pluto," was his polite way of rejecting her.

Andrea scowled and looked morose for a moment but then brightened and turned to me. To avoid her impending pleas for money, I pretended to be fascinated with a fly crawling on the wall. "You'll both be sorry when I'm rich and famous," Andrea cried, and stormed out of the room. When we last saw her, she was fingerprinting the dog, whose compliance was more to her liking.

1. _____ singular _____ unusual, extraordinary

2. _____ dispelled _____ driven away or scattered

3. _____ impending _____ soon to happen, coming

4. _____ bequeathed _____ left or gave to someone, as in a will

5. _____ defray _____ to pay

6. _____ compliance _____ yielding to another's wishes

7. _____ allusion _____ mention of or reference to something

8. _____ morose _____ gloomy, ill-humored

THE SPECKLED BAND

Name _____

Fill in the story chart. **Accept reasonable responses.**

SETTING: **London; Stoke Moran**

CHARACTERS: **Holmes, Watson, Helen Stoner, Dr. Roylott, Julia Stoner**

PREDICTION: **Responses will vary.**

EVENT	CLUES	PREDICTION
1. **Helen Stoner visits Holmes.**	whistle clang speckled band	
2. **Roylott visits Holmes.**	Roylott's temper the will	
3. **Holmes and Watson go to Stoke Moran.**	bell rope ventilator bed	
4. **Holmes solves the mystery.**	leash milk	

SOLUTION: **Roylott trained a swamp adder in order to murder Julia.**

Summarizing the Literature

• • • THE SPECKLED BAND • • •

Name _____

Read the following description of Helen Stoner in "The Speckled Band," and think about the conclusions you can draw about her character from the description. Then complete the exercises. **Responses will vary.**

> Helen Stoner has been devastated by the death of her sister, Julia. She holds back evidence of her stepfather's violence toward her. She knows she is in danger because, as her sister was, she is engaged to be married, and she is sleeping in Julia's old room. She has come to Sherlock Holmes to see whether he can help her.

1. Write a one-sentence conclusion about Helen Stoner's feelings for her sister. Give evidence from the description.

Helen was a loving sister to Julia. Evidence: She is devastated by Julia's

death.

2. Write a one-sentence conclusion about Helen Stoner's behavior toward her stepfather. Give evidence from the description.

Helen is forgiving of her stepfather's behavior and protective of his

reputation. Evidence: She does not let anyone know that he has been violent

toward her.

3. Write a one-sentence conclusion about Helen Stoner's attitude toward herself and her own safety. Give evidence from the description.

Helen is realistic and smart about her situation. Evidence: She recognizes

that her current position is much like her sister's before Julia died, and she

seeks out someone with the skill to help her solve the mystery.

SUMMARIZING *the* **L**EARNING

A conclusion is a _____**judgment**_____ inferred or deduced from evidence. To draw a conclusion, a reader uses both the _____**facts**_____ in a story and his or her _____**personal**_____ _____**experience**_____.

Name _____

Read the passage below, and then number the events in the order in which they happened in real time.

A Night of Watching

Mario crept through the marsh grass, stopping every so often to listen to the wind. It brought him sounds of the water and of boats bumping against the pier, but no human sounds. He did not have to be afraid, at least not yet. He clutched his flashlight to his chest.

Mario lay quietly by the shore, his eyes on the darkened boat shed. He remembered how shocked he had been several hours earlier when he was walking toward the shed and saw two men crouched alongside. They were wrapping a package in waterproof plastic and whispering to each other. Mario had recognized them from a news photo he had seen in the paper a week previously. They were escaped bank robbers. He had been sure they were hiding the bank loot in his family's boat shed.

Now Mario crouched lower as he heard soft footsteps approaching. His father, Alphonso, was creeping along the beach with two uniformed police. Suddenly, there was a creak from the boat-shed door, and the two robbers ran silently through the door and down the beach. Mario stood up and shined the flashlight on them, pinning them down. After a brief scuffle, the police apprehended them, while Mario and his father watched.

_____2_____ Mario saw the bank robbers wrapping something in plastic at his family's boat shed.

_____4_____ Alphonso and the police crept up to the boat shed.

_____6_____ The police caught the bank robbers.

_____3_____ Mario crouched in the grass, watching the shed.

_____1_____ Mario saw the bank robbers' picture in the newspaper.

_____5_____ The robbers ran out of the shed.

SUMMARIZING the LEARNING

Sequence refers to the order in which events __happened__, not the order in which they are __revealed__.

Name _____

Read the selection on these two pages. As you read, fill in the details that support each statement.

DETAILS

It is important for Butler to complete his investigation soon. **It will rain soon and wash away any tracks.**

Ben Ebert hopes his cattle were taken by coyotes. **He will be compensated if coyotes took his calves.**

Butler had difficulty telling which tracks were which. **Many animals used the trail.**

Butler has difficulty doing his work. **He has a bad back.**

Wildlife ranger Harry Butler pulled into the yard of Rancher Ben Ebert and scanned the horizon. More rain coming, he thought. Will wash out any tracks that the cattle might have left. Good thing I got here before the heavens open.

Ebert was waiting for the ranger. A huge, bluff man with a perpetually red face, he shifted impatiently from foot to foot as he watched Butler approach him. "Darned coyotes again," he spat in an overly loud voice. "We'll have to kill them all, Butler, or this won't be a fit place to raise cattle."

"We've been through this before, Ebert," Harry sighed. "If coyotes have taken your young calves, you'll be compensated. But you know we did that study last year that showed only a few calves were taken over an area of several states. The rest were stolen, wandered off, or died of natural causes."

"Hmpffh," snarled Ebert. He watched as Butler started off down the trail, following the path animals would likely take into the deeper canyon country. Eyes to the ground, Butler had trouble distinguishing all the different tracks on the often-used path. And his bad back made it difficult to bend over.

Name _____

After a mile or two, Butler came to a dry wash. It had filled and rushed with water during the rain yesterday but was now just wet bottom land. He crossed it and found the remains of a large campfire and evidence of much activity. Boot heels were mixed in with cattle tracks, but it was hard to figure out how many of each. Butler rummaged through the rubble and discovered a hat, a dirty scarf, and several empty food tins. Then his eagle eyes spotted a thick chunk of metal near the campfire. As he picked it up he whistled. "Oh, ho, coyotes, you have increased your skills since last we met."

When Butler limped back into Ebert's yard, the old rancher was gazing at him smugly. He sprawled on the bottom step and did not even get up. "Found the carcasses, did ye?" he drawled. "When will I get my money?"

"Nope," replied Butler. "But I did find this," and he handed Ebert the metal object. It was in the shape of a **Y** with a curve below it; a thick rod of metal extended from it a short distance, then broke off suddenly. "Last time I looked, coyotes weren't able to brand cattle," said Butler. "This is an abandoned brand. Apparently the thieves broke it while they were working and forgot to take it along. We need to find a ranch in the area that has a rocking-Y brand."

"Now, mind you," he added, straight-faced, as Ebert looked as if he would burst, "if it turns out that the cattle rustlers are a bunch of branding coyotes, well, I'm sure we can compensate you for your cattle. Good day to you, sir."

DETAILS

A dry wash can be dangerous at times.
It was filled and rushing during the rain.

Human beings have been at the scene.
Butler finds campfire remains, boot tracks, hat, scarf, food tins.

Ebert doesn't have much respect for Butler.
He does not stand up and speaks casually.

What will the missing calves look like?
They will have a brand in the shape of a rocking-Y.

The Great Peanut Puzzle

Name _____

Complete the story by writing a word from the box on each line. Then write each word on the line next to its meaning.

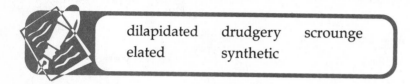

| dilapidated | drudgery | scrounge |
| elated | synthetic | |

My cousins Jackie and Monroe are geniuses. They really are. They go to a school that doesn't have much money for science classes.

The science room had turned into a ___**dilapidated**___ mess after years of neglect. But Jackie and Monroe decided to restock it.

They asked all their classmates to ___**scrounge**___ around at home and bring in whatever they could spare—cups, saucers, pots and pans, remains of old chemistry sets, anything! Then they all

grumbled and groaned their way through the ___**drudgery**___ of cleaning up the room and making it usable. The last I heard, they

were ___**elated**___ because they had discovered a new substance that could replace plastic and would not be bad for the environment. Since it is made artificially, they are calling it the

"___**Synthetic**___ Substance."

1. ___**drudgery**___ tiresome work

2. ___**synthetic**___ made in a laboratory

3. ___**dilapidated**___ fallen into ruin or disrepair

4. ___**scrounge**___ to search for or beg

5. ___**elated**___ overjoyed

Name _____

Fill in the SQ3R chart. **Accept reasonable responses.**

SURVEY This selection is about how George Washington Carver solved some mysteries.		
QUESTION	PREDICTED ANSWER	READ
What is the great peanut puzzle?		

RECITE	REVIEW

• • • THE GREAT PEANUT PUZZLE • • •

Name _____

Use context clues to determine the meaning of each underlined word in the paragraphs. Then complete each numbered sentence by writing the correct definition on the line. Choose from the four listed.

George Washington Carver was a specialist in the science of botany, which includes the study of peanuts and cotton. When he first arrived at Tuskegee Institute, to teach agricultural science, the laboratory was a disaster. Without microscopes to observe tiny plant cells, it was impossible to do experiments to find new agricultural methods.

After Carver assembled a laboratory, he showed farmers how to improve their cotton crops by restoring nitrogen from the air to the soil. Next, he worked with peanuts. Shoe polish, shampoo, and paper were just a few of the synthetic products he created from peanut mixtures. Carver was truly a scientific genius.

1. *Botany* is the **study of plants** _____ .

    study of animals   study of plants
    study of peanuts   study of cotton

2. A *laboratory* is a **place to do scientific work** _____ .

    place to wash hands   place to observe stars
    place to do scientific work   place to sell peanuts

3. *Agricultural* means "having to do with **farming** _____ ."

    fishing   farming
    cooking   advertising

4. A *microscope* is an instrument to **make objects look larger** _____ .

    make objects look larger   make objects look smaller
    make objects disappear   make objects move

5. *Nitrogen* is a **gas found in the air** _____ .

    kind of soil   type of cotton
    crop   gas found in the air

6. *Synthetic* means " **made artificially** _____ ."

    made from peanuts   made artificially
    made under a microscope   made from plant cells

••• THE GREAT PEANUT PUZZLE •••

Name _____

Read the passage, and answer the questions.

A. The practice of using irrigation on farms in order to grow food for humans
can have devastating effects on wildlife. For example, people redirected
the streams that used to fill California's Mono Lake, which was a haven for
birds as well as for fish and other aquatic life. The water level in the lake
fell 45 feet, killing most of the aquatic life. Therefore, the flocks of birds
that fed off the aquatic life eventually shrank.

1. What caused wildlife in Mono Lake to diminish? __**In order to irrigate their fields,**__
__**people redirected the streams that filled the lake. The water level fell, killing**__
__**most of the lake's aquatic life.**__

2. What effect did the fall of Mono Lake's water level have on the birds? __**The fish were**__
__**killed, so the number of birds that fed there shrank.**__

_____

B. Environmental awareness in the 1990s is making people think twice about
their living habits. The growing amount of garbage is leading them to the
recycling of paper and plastics. New evidence of the ozone layer's
depletion is making the use of aerosol sprays practically nonexistent. The
world of the 1990s will be dramatically different from any known before.

1. What two things are causing people to change their living habits? __**the growing amount**__
__**of garbage and new evidence of the depletion of the ozone layer**__

2. What effect is environmental awareness having on people of the 1990s? __**It is causing**__
__**them to re-evaluate their living habits.**__

_____

SUMMARIZING
the **L**EARNING   If one _____**event**_____ causes another event to happen, this is a
_____**cause-and-effect**_____ relationship.

HBJ material copyrighted under notice appearing earlier in this work.

Name _____

Read the selection, and complete the exercises.

Matthew sat straight in his chair, his mind racing. He was barely aware of the other students sitting near him, coughing, shifting in their seats, and generally acting just as nervous as he was. *Metronome*, he thought suddenly. And then—*propeller*—remember -er, not -or. Several more words swirled through his mind. Uh-oh, he thought, *isthmus*. He had had trouble with that one last evening when his sister was quizzing him.

1. Based on your prior knowledge and the information in the selection, what do you think is going on here?

Matthew has been studying words, and so have the other kids. I predict that

he is about to take a spelling test or has entered a spelling bee.

The tester walked on stage. "Ready, spellers?" he said grinning. "Let's go. First up." A girl on the end walked to the microphone. "*Rendezvous*," announced the tester.

"*Rendezvous*." She cleared her throat. "R-E-N-D-E-Z-V . . . O-U-S."

"Correct," called the tester. The girl blushed and sat down. A boy got up next. Matthew knew him from school. "*Dissident*," chanted the tester.

"*Dissident*," the boy mumbled. "D-I-S-S-E-D-E-N-T."

"I'm sorry, that is incorrect," said the tester. The boy walked off, head down. Now it was Matthew's turn!

"*Retrorocket*," sang out the tester. Matthew froze. He hadn't studied this word. But he was an amateur astronomer and a space-travel fanatic. He walked confidently to the microphone.

2. What do you think will happen next?

Matthew has not studied the word but has probably run across it in his

reading about space travel. I predict he will spell it correctly.

SUMMARIZING *the* **L**EARNING   When you make predictions, you use _____**prior knowledge**_____

and _____**information**_____ from the selection to guess what will happen.

• • • THE GREAT PEANUT PUZZLE • • •

Name _____

Read about each research project below. Then decide which of the following sources you would use to complete each project: dictionary, encyclopedia, atlas, card catalog, almanac, *Books in Print*, *Readers' Guide to Periodical Literature*, computer data base. What topics would you look up in each reference source?

1. PROJECT—A report on the discoveries made by the *Voyager* spacecraft about the planets Jupiter, Saturn, Uranus, and Neptune between 1980 and 1989. Reports should include what information scientists knew about the planets before the *Voyager* project and what they learned because of the *Voyager* project. It should also include photographs.

Use *Books in Print*, card catalog, and computer data base to find titles of

recent books; encyclopedia articles; and *Readers' Guide* for current articles.

Look under topics *Voyager*, *Space Travel*, and the names of the planets.

2. PROJECT—A report on the civilizations of the Huron and Iroquois Indians in North America at the time the French settlers arrived. The report should include information on words taken into English from these Indian languages. It should also show maps of land use before and after the French arrived.

Use *Books in Print*, computer data base, and card catalog to find titles of

books; encyclopedia articles. Look under topics *Huron Indians*, *Iroquois*

***Indians*, *American Indians*, *Exploration*, *French*, and *English Language*. Use**

an unabridged dictionary to check etymologies for words mentioned in

other sources as being taken from Huron and Iroquois languages. Use

historical atlas to find maps showing North America before and after French

arrival.

Name _____

Read the following paragraphs. Use clues in the passage to determine the meaning of each underlined word. Then write each word on the line next to its meaning.

Sleep is a common phenomenon that most people experience for several hours each day. Ironically, as common as it is, we do not understand sleep very well. Scientists have, however, learned some important things about sleep. It is absolutely necessary for mental as well as physical health. People who get too little sleep become disoriented. They have trouble thinking or speaking coherently.

Have you noticed that a dream may seem so real that it's hard to believe it is only an illusion? Many people remember speaking very lucid language in dreams, only to realize later on that they were speaking gibberish. An important thing about regular sleeping and dreaming is that it revitalizes us; it makes us like new.

1. _____coherently_____ logically or sensibly

2. _____illusion_____ something unreal that appears to be real

3. _____phenomenon_____ fact or event that can be observed

4. _____lucid_____ clear and understandable

5. _____ironically_____ surprisingly, or in an unexpected way

6. _____revitalizes_____ restores

7. _____disoriented_____ confused and frightened

Name _____

Complete the K-W-L chart. **Responses will vary.**

K *What I Know*	W *What I Want to Know*	L *What I Learned*
People sleep every night.		

Name _____

Read each selection on these two pages, and complete the exercise that goes with it. Then complete the exercise at the end of all the selections.

THE DAILY BLAT
Springville, November 16, 1991

Doctors and psychologists in Springville have noted an increase in sleep disorders during the past two years. "More and more of my patients are complaining that they either sleep too much or too little," said Dr. Martha Psyche. "I'm concerned because it does not appear to be organic, and I dislike just giving pills to everybody."

Dr. Seth O. Scope reported that he prescribes warm milk for 2 out of every 4 patients these days. "No matter what else is wrong with folks, they also seem to have sleeping problems," he sighed. "Actually, I'm waking up a lot in the night, myself."

Information from Different Sources

Write a main idea you learned from this source.

Doctors and psychologists in a city are reporting an increase in sleep disorders, which has occurred over two years.

FORMAL PRESS RELEASE

From: Springville Employment Bureau
To: All Local Newspaper, TV, and Radio Reporters

The State Employment Bureau announced today that unemployment has risen another 2.5 percent during the year. Plant closings, companies that relocate to foreign countries, and the basic poor condition of the economy were cited as reasons. "This will mean more homelessness, more illness, and more crime," said an official. "And it looks as if it will be a while before the condition changes."

What important cause-and-effect idea did you learn here?

Unemployment continues to rise, and officials fear this will lead to more illness and crime.

THE GREAT SHUT-EYE MYSTERY

Name _____

Sleep

Many factors affect a person's sleeping patterns. Some people sleep long hours to escape from stress, while others react to pressure in their daily lives by becoming insomniacs, people unable to sleep.

Cory wasn't asleep when the fire broke out. He hadn't slept well for weeks because he was concerned about the farm and his father's seeming disapproval of him. When he saw the flames, he ran to the barn. Only he could save the horses; they would panic if anyone else tried to move them. As if in a dream, he saw himself burst through the door and make his way to the stalls. Ginger and Buckwheat, blind with fear, sensed him and quieted and then let him lead them to safety.

Cory's father praised him to the stars. "I had no idea you were so responsible, son," he apologized. "Things will be different between us now; you can count on it." Cory slept well that night.

What important information did you learn in this source?

Stress causes some people to escape by sleeping and others to become insomniacs.

Summarize this short passage by writing about the main ideas.

Cory was worried about many things and did not sleep well. One night, lying awake, he saw the barn burning. He ran bravely into the building and saved the two horses. Pleased by his father's praise, Cory slept well that night.

Based on all the selections you have read and the main ideas you have listed, write a short conclusion that combines all this information.

Accept reasonable responses: Stress of various kinds appears to affect sleeping patterns. The stress can be social, such as unemployment and homelessness, or personal, such as problems in family relationships. Some people react to stress by oversleeping and others by not being able to sleep at all.

Name _____

Read each section of the selection, and complete the exercise that goes with it.

The scientists walked quickly into the hotel. They noted the frightened looks on the faces of many guests who were huddled in the lobby. The hotel manager ran to them and sputtered, "Please, we want you to meet with our hotel doctor. It happened so suddenly. One person became ill in one part of the hotel, and then several others in a different part. It happened in the middle of the afternoon. Some people were still in meetings, and others were relaxing. No one was eating anything, except for packaged snacks such as peanuts and chips. It . . . was . . . so . . . strange!" he panted.

Three of the scientists interviewed the ill guests, while others began to move through the hotel, checking the places where people had become sick. Hours passed, and a few more people were stricken. "We can't let anyone leave until we know what it is, or we could have a citywide epidemic on our hands," said one scientist. Suddenly, one of the scientists hurried into the manager's office. "Get me a diagram of the hotel's heating and air conditioning system," he demanded. "Where the air passages are, which of them lead to which rooms—all that information. Quickly!" Mystified, the manager rushed off to comply.

Based on your prior knowledge and what you have learned so far, what do you think is going on here? What will the scientists have to figure out? What possibility can they probably rule out already?

People are being stricken by some illness. Scientists will have to figure out how it is being spread. It is probably not food poisoning, because several people became ill at the same time, and people were not eating any prepared food.

What do you predict will happen next?
Responses will vary. The scientists will find that what caused the illness is traveling through the hotel's ventilation system. All the people infected will be found to have been in areas serviced by the same parts of the system.

Name _____

Read the list of reference sources. Then answer the questions. Tell which reference sources you would use and where you would look in each one.

Books in Print   *Readers' Guide to Periodical Literature*   an atlas

A. You are preparing a paper on endangered species in other countries. You want to focus on Africa and South America.

1. Where would you look to determine the sizes of both continents and to see what kinds of landforms there are in each?
Look in an atlas to find topographical maps of both countries.

2. Where would you look to find sources that might include substantial information on the plight of elephants in Kenya and jaguars in the South American rain forests?
Look in *Books in Print* under subjects: Conservation, Endangered Species,

Africa, Kenya, South America, Rain Forests, Elephant, and Jaguar.

B. You are preparing a report on the kinds of natural resources found in Alaska and Hawaii.

1. Where would you look to find graphic information on what products and resources are found in each state?
Use an atlas to find product and resource maps of the states.

2. Where would you look to find sources for how these resources were used before the states became part of the United States, and how they are used today?
Look in *Books in Print* under subjects: Alaska, History of and Natural

Resources of; Hawaii, History of and Natural Resources of; *Readers' Guide*

for recent articles on Alaska and Hawaii, under the subheads Crops and

Natural Resources.

••• M.C. Higgins, the Great •••

Name _____

A. Read the sentences. Underline the correct meaning for the boldface word in each sentence.

1. Jennie **slithered** down the bank and into the lake as if she were an otter.

    crept   <u>slid</u>   ran   dived

2. She had always been a terrific swimmer, as **attuned** to the watery environment as a fish.

    out of tune with   afraid   allergic   <u>in harmony with</u>

3. I don't like water and actually **cringed** once when I got near the lake.

    <u>shuddered in fear</u>   laughed   fell in   pouted

4. Several times I tried **futilely** to learn to swim.

    successfully   <u>unsuccessfully</u>   furiously   happily

5. I'd like to reach that **serene** and happy state that Jennie feels when she is in the water, but I wonder whether it will ever happen.

    deep   cold   wet   <u>calm</u>

B. Use each of the five boldface words in a sentence of your own. **Students' sentences will vary.**

1. _____

_____

2. _____

_____

3. _____

_____

4. _____

_____

5. _____

• • • M.C. HIGGINS, THE GREAT • • •

Name _____

Complete the sequence diagram. **Accept reasonable responses.**

CHARACTERS/SETTING

How does the selection begin?
M.C., children, and girl are at the lake.

ACTIONS/EVENTS

What happens first?
M.C. and girl discuss tunnel.

ACTIONS/EVENTS

What happens next?
They go through the tunnel and almost don't make it.

ACTIONS/EVENTS

What happens last?
M.C. and girl argue and make up.

RESOLUTION

How do the characters feel about each other at the end?
M.C. and girl respect each other.

TIME SPAN

How much time passes altogether?
about an hour or less

Name _____

Read the following selection on these two pages, and complete the exercises.

Today Doris was more frantic than usual. The plans for her parents' wedding anniversary were not going smoothly. Perhaps she should not have agreed to supervise the preparations; after all, she was only fourteen. But her parents' friends all worked long hours, and it would be hard for them to be involved in the planning. Doris quickly stashed the groceries she had bought for the party on a top shelf, where her mother would not be likely to see them. Then she went back to her worrying. Her parents' friends would contribute food, gifts, and money, but it was up to Doris to get everything set up.

Now, if she could only count on her younger sister and brother— she called them the Celebrity and the Couch Potato, respectively. At this point Doris was hurriedly stuffing the decorations under her bed as she thought about her siblings. Her sister, Margo, was already an accomplished ice skater at age ten. She had won a half-dozen awards and had appeared in shows with famous skaters and other well-known people, about whom she talked incessantly. "So-and-so said this to me," was her favorite saying at the moment, using the nickname of a sports celebrity. Actually, Doris had to give Margo credit: the kid was a good skater. And she managed to do it while maintaining an A average in school. She and Doris got along most of the time, but when Margo started boasting about all her famous friends, Doris wanted to gag.

As for her brother, Rick, he had too many friends. They were always at the apartment watching TV, eating the family's food, and in general being a pain. How someone who watched so much television could have such good friends was a mystery to Doris. Maybe he had a secret life apart from the family, one that she didn't know about, kind of like Superman.

Name _____

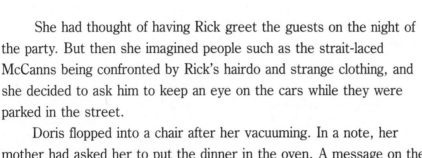

She had thought of having Rick greet the guests on the night of the party. But then she imagined people such as the strait-laced McCanns being confronted by Rick's hairdo and strange clothing, and she decided to ask him to keep an eye on the cars while they were parked in the street.

Doris flopped into a chair after her vacuuming. In a note, her mother had asked her to put the dinner in the oven. A message on the phone machine from her father told her he appreciated the books she had brought him from the library yesterday. She rarely saw her parents because of their long working hours. Was that what she, Margo, and Rick had to look forward to—long, hard work during the best hours of the day? Well, she had too much to worry about now to start worrying about the future.

1. Which characters in this story are rounded? Why? **Doris, her brother, Rick, and her sister, Margo, are rounded characters. We know the most about Doris and what she thinks and feels, and we know some of these things about Rick and Margo, too.**

2. Which characters are flat? Why? **The children's parents are flat characters. We know nothing about them except that they work hard.**

3. What is the mood of the story? What kind of feeling does the author create? **The mood is energetic, frazzled, and frantic.**

4. What is the tone of the story? What attitude does the author have toward the characters and the material? **The author takes a humorous, casual tone toward the material.**

Name _____

Read the stories, and answer the questions.

A.   Raisa and Tina were good friends and very much alike. They each
liked to outdo the other. If Raisa got an A in science, Tina would try to get
an A+ in math. If Tina made the varsity soccer team, Raisa would work
hard to be on the basketball team. In addition, they both loved the
outdoors.
    One day they were hiking along a new trail. They came to a washed-
out area. The distance from one side to the other was more than 5 feet.
The girls looked at each other.

1. What conclusion can you draw about Raisa and Tina's friendship?

They are good friends, but they are also competitors.

2. What do you predict will happen next in the story? Why?

Accept reasonable responses. Both girls will try to jump the gap.

B.   Sam helped his younger brother and sister cross the street. He had
helped care for his younger siblings since he was ten, because his parents
trusted him. Now they were headed for Mr. Stone's hardware store. "Be
careful. Watch for cars," he warned them.
    As Sam went to the counter to ask for help, the younger children ran off
to look at the merchandise. Suddenly there was a loud crash. Sam rushed
over to find Mr. Stone standing over a pile of broken glass. "He broke that
lantern while he was trying to steal it!" thundered Mr. Stone, towering over
Sam's brother.

1. What conclusion can you draw about Sam's character?

He is capable and responsible.

2. What do you predict will happen next? Why?

Accept reasonable responses: Sam will insist that the broken glass was an

accident, not a theft, and will offer to pay for the item. Sam trusts his

brother, and he is also responsible enough to know that someone has to

pay for the damage.

• • • M.C. Higgins, the Great • • •

Name _____

Read each pair of events, and mark each event *1st* or *2nd* to show the
order in which they happened. Then write a sentence to explain the cause-
and-effect relationship between the two events. Explain *why* the second
event follows the first event.

1. _____**2nd**_____ M.C. Higgins dives into a pool and swims through a tunnel.

   _____**1st**_____ The Higgins children meet a new girl at the lake.

   M.C. dives into the pool and swims through the tunnel because he wants to

   impress the newcomer.

2. _____**1st**_____ The girl keeps looking at the pool and the rocks.

   _____**2nd**_____ M.C. asks the girl how long she can hold her breath.

   M.C. asks the girl how long she can hold her breath because he can see she

   is interested in going through the tunnel.

3. _____**1st**_____ In the tunnel, the girl is like a dead weight to M.C.

   _____**2nd**_____ M.C. bangs his knees on the bottom of the tunnel.

   M.C. bangs his knees, because the girl cannot swim and drags him down in

   the tunnel.

4. _____**2nd**_____ The Higgins children are shocked.

   _____**1st**_____ The girl brags that she went through the tunnel without knowing
   how to swim.

   The Higgins children are shocked because they cannot believe the girl would

   do such a foolish thing.

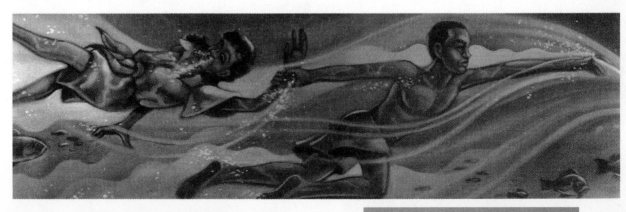

••• A RETRIEVED REFORMATION •••

Name _____

A. Read the sentences. Underline the words that explain or give clues to the meaning of the boldface word.

1. With awe and respect, the jury watched quietly as the **eminent** Lost-Boy-turned-lawyer, Peter Pan, walked up to the witness stand.

2. The **elusive** Captain Hook had finally been caught.

3. "Do you deny that you have spent your life capturing helpless Lost Boys and attempting to convert them to a life of crime, and that you did this through the use of cunning, with **guile** in your heart?" asked Pan.

4. "Objection!" shouted the defense lawyer. "You have made two **specious** comments already: the Lost Boys have never been helpless, and Captain Hook has no heart!"

5. As if to mock the proceedings, Hook hooted, "You only want to see me locked up to get back at me for allowing you to get away and grow up! It's a simple case of a little boy seeking **retribution**!"

6. Pan turned to the jury. "Surely you are not going to grant **clemency** to this villain, who obviously deserves the opposite: your harshest judgment!"

7. "Order in the court!" shouted the judge. "Remember, this court's job is to decide whether to **rehabilitate** Captain James Hook by giving him a job in an orphanage and restoring him to moral health!"

8. Closely watching each speaker, the court reporter **assiduously** recorded every word spoken in the courtroom.

B. Choose four of the boldface words, and use each in a sentence of your own on another sheet of paper.
Sentences will vary.

••• A RETRIEVED REFORMATION •••

Name _____

Complete the story plot map. **Accept reasonable responses.**

PROBLEM

Jimmy Valentine is a bank robber who will not reform.

RISING ACTION

EVENT

Detective Ben Price starts to track Jimmy.

EVENT

Jimmy falls in love with Annabel and gives up crime.

EVENT

Ben Price arrives in Elmore.

CLIMAX

To save a child locked in a safe, Jimmy must reveal that he is a safecracker.

RESOLUTION

Seeing Jimmy's selfless act, Ben Price decides not to arrest him.

Events students choose to include in Rising Action may vary.

••• A RETRIEVED REFORMATION •••

Name _____

Read each passage from "A Retrieved Reformation" on these two pages. Then answer the inference questions.

A. He had served nearly ten months of a four-year sentence. He had expected to stay only about three months, at the longest. When a man with as many friends on the outside as Jimmy Valentine had is received in the "stir" it is hardly worthwhile to cut his hair.

1. What is the "stir"? What words help you infer this? __The "stir" is prison. It is implied by__.
__the whole passage, but especially in the sentence "He had served nearly ten__
__months of a four-year sentence."__

2. How would a person like Jimmy Valentine expect to get out of prison early?
__His friends on the outside would find a way to get him out.__

3. How did you arrive at your answer for the second question?
__Accept reasonable responses: I know that sometimes well-connected friends__
__can pull strings for someone, and the writer notes that for someone with as__
__many friends as Jimmy has, it is hardly worthwhile cutting his hair, meaning__
__that such a person would not be likely to remain in prison long.__

B. "Sorry we couldn't make it sooner, Jimmy, me boy," said Mike. "But we had that protest from Springfield to buck against, and the governor nearly balked. Feeling all right?"

1. Did Mike have anything to do with Jimmy's release from jail?
__Yes.__ What words help you infer this? __"Sorry we couldn't make it sooner, Jimmy,__
__me boy," and "the governor nearly balked."__

2. What do you think was being protested? __Accept reasonable responses:__
__People didn't want Jimmy set free.__

••• A RETRIEVED REFORMATION •••

Name _____

C. Jimmy Valentine looked into her eyes, forgot what he was, and became another man. She lowered her eyes and colored slightly. Young men of Jimmy's style and looks were scarce in Elmore.

1. What does Jimmy think of the young woman? __He likes her.__

2. What does the young lady think of Jimmy? __She is impressed.__

3. How did you make the inferences you did? __Accept reasonable responses:__
Seeing the young woman makes him want to forget that he has lived a life of

crime and be a better person. People blush when they're caught looking at

someone they like, and since men as nice-looking as Jimmy are rare in

Elmore, she is probably staring.

D. While they were thus engaged Ben Price sauntered in and leaned on his elbow, looking casually inside between the railings. He told the teller that he didn't want anything; he was just waiting for a man he knew.

1. How does Ben feel as he enters the bank? What words help you infer this? __He feels__
calm and sure of himself. The words "sauntered in," "leaned on his elbow,"

and "looking casually" make him appear calm and self-assured.

2. At this point in the story, what did you think Ben was going to do? Why? __Accept__
reasonable responses: He is there to arrest Jimmy Valentine because he's taken

a good look at Spencer and recognized him. Also, Ben's goal in life seems to be

to put Valentine behind bars.

••• A RETRIEVED REFORMATION •••

Name _____

Read the passage, and then complete the exercise. Use your own words and ideas, as well as those from the passage, to complete each sentence. Then circle either *CAUSE* or *EFFECT* to show which part you added.

Officer Hinton stepped out of his patrol car and stood next to the disabled school bus. "Looks like you're having some trouble," he said.

"We sure are," said Coach Williams. "We have a game at Clancy High School at seven o'clock, and I'm not sure we can make it. Do you think we can get some water somewhere? The engine's overheating." The members of Jackson High's football team gathered beside the bus and looked hopefully at the patrolman.

"I'll run and pick some up," he said. "You should be back on the road in thirty minutes."

Coach Williams looked at his watch. "Guys," he said, looking at his team, "I think we may have to forfeit this one."

"That means we lose the division," Jordan whispered to Greg.

Greg nodded. "We beat Clancy last time, too. I know we could have won again tonight!"

Officer Hinton picked up his radio. "I'll phone ahead and let 'em know you're on your way. My guess is they'll be happy to hold the kick-off for you." He smiled. "My son plays right tackle for Clancy. He'd sure hate to have this game canceled—he wants a chance to beat you fair and square!"

1. The bus is disabled because **its engine is overheating.**
(CAUSE)   EFFECT

2. Since the team is going to be late, Coach Williams figures **it will have to forfeit the game.**

CAUSE   (EFFECT)

3. If the team loses the game tonight, **it will lose the division championship.**
CAUSE   (EFFECT)

4. Officer Hinton thinks the Clancy team will hold the game for Jackson High because **the team members will want a chance to beat Jackson fair and square.**

(CAUSE)   EFFECT

••• A RETRIEVED REFORMATION •••

Name _____

Read the story opening and answer the questions.

Trouble in Stonecliff City

There never was a time that year when the Bank of Stonecliff City seemed safe. Oh, it was built to withstand just about anything. It had doors thick enough to hold off a herd of buffalo, and a safe with more locks than the schoolmarm had reasons to give what-for to Bucky Burdock. It had those high ceilings bank presidents seem to like. I always figured the fella who designed 'em thought if a bank looked enough like a New York City church, no bandit would have the gumption to rob it.

But they broke into it anyway—not just the Hixton boys, but the Raw Creek Gang, the Peabodies, and Ma Drake as well, all between April and September. Nobody knew how they managed it, not until one fall night when the night watchman happened to be awake instead of asleep. He wasn't a hero. Guess nobody in Stonecliff City was that. But he did solve the mystery. And thanks to him, we all know just how the Spencer Family got away off to Mexico with the last $4.54 any of us felt comfortable leaving in the vault of the majestic Bank of Stonecliff City.

1. What is the setting of the story?

a. Time: **Sometime during the days of the Old West** _____

b. Place: **Stonecliff City, somewhere in the Old West** _____

2. Is the setting implied or stated? If implied, what words led to your conclusion? **The place is stated three times, implied by the kind of language used, such as *bandit, figured, schoolmarm,* and *gumption,* and the kinds of comparisons made, such as "more locks than the schoolmarm had reasons to give what-for to Bucky Burdock."**

3. What might you expect to happen in a story with such a setting?
Accept reasonable responses: The bank will be robbed.

• • • MOTHER AND DAUGHTER • • •

Name _____

A. Read the following sentences. Use the context clues to determine the meaning of each underlined word. Write each underlined word on the line next to its definition.

1. My brother delivered another <u>tirade</u> this morning, lecturing us on our laziness.

2. Sometimes he gets so angry that I think he will explode and overflow like <u>molten</u> lava from a volcano.

3. He apparently was particularly disturbed by our playful <u>antics</u> during the time when we were supposed to be cleaning the house.

4. My brother needs to loosen up, because he has a <u>meager</u> sense of humor.

pranks or tricks _____**antics**_____

poor or small _____**meager**_____

long and angry speech _____**tirade**_____

melted by great heat _____**molten**_____

B. Read each question. Write your answer on the line, or place a check in the box in front of the answer. There may be more than one correct answer.

1. If someone is delivering a tirade, would you want to stay near that person? _____**no**_____

   Explain your answer. _____**Accept reasonable responses: I would leave someone**

   who is yelling at me._____

2. Which of these items might you consider meager?
   ☐ a pot of gold   ☑ a penny   ☐ a thousand dollars

3. Which of these actions might have something to do with antics?
   ☑ tying someone's shoelaces in knots   ☑ spraying someone with a garden hose
   ☐ doing homework   ☐ going to a baseball game

4. What machine might create molten substances?
   ☐ a television   ☐ a refrigerator   ☑ a furnace

MOTHER AND DAUGHTER

Name _____

Complete the character traits chart to summarize "Mother and Daughter."
Accept reasonable responses. Possible answers are provided.

CHARACTERS	YOLLIE	MRS. MORENO
Different	young raised in U.S.A.	older raised in Mexico
Alike	sense of humor	

Name _____

Read these Spanish words and phrases that are commonly used in English. Practice saying them by using the pronunciations provided. Use a standard dictionary, a Spanish-English dictionary, or the glossary of a Spanish language textbook to fill in their meanings.

	Spanish	Pronunciation	Meaning
1.	Buenas noches.	bwā′näs nō′ches	**good evening, good night**
2.	plaza	plä′sä	**a town square**
3.	fiesta	fē·es′tä	**a celebration or festival**
4.	adobe	ə·dō′bā	**sun dried bricks of clay and straw**
5.	mañana	mä·nyä′nä	**tomorrow**
6.	Mucho gusto.	mo͞o′chō go͞o′stō	**Nice to meet you.**
7.	¿Que pasa?	kā pä′sä	**What's going on?**
8.	chili	chē′lā	**a sharp-flavored fruit that makes a spicy seasoning**
9.	sierra	sē·yä′rä	**mountain range with an irregular or sawtoothed appearance**

Buenas noches.

See you mañana!

• • • MOTHER AND DAUGHTER • • •

Name _____

Use context clues to determine the meaning of the underlined word in each sentence or pair of sentences. Circle any word or words that offer clues to the meaning. Then put a (✔) next to the correct meaning.

1. As they entered the arena, the throbbing music of the band reverberated under their feet and filled their ears like the heartbeat of a gigantic animal.

  ✔ loud, heavy and resounding   ☐ soft, relaxing   ☐ strange, new

2. Samantha awakened from her dream, but she had been so deeply asleep that her grogginess caused her to stumble out of bed.

  ☐ clumsiness   ☐ excitement   ✔ dazed or half-conscious condition

3. Janet was angry at her brother's treatment of her. She gloated with satisfaction when the older boys rejected him from their group.

  ✔ took pleasure in someone else's discomfort or pain
  ☐ felt sorry for someone else
  ☐ smiled

4. Kevin counted his few pennies and dimes. Such a meager amount would never be enough to buy Susan a present.

  ☐ great   ✔ small   ☐ satisfactory

5. Luisa looked at her simple dress and shoes and knew she would be outshined by Maria's sophisticated attire.

  ☐ similar   ☐ new   ✔ worldly or cultured

6. As they walked from the car to the dance, it began to pour down rain, and by the time they reached the door their clothing was drenched.

  ✔ soaked   ☐ wrinkled   ☐ ruined

SUMMARIZING *the* **L**EARNING   In order to figure out the _____**meaning**_____ of a new or unfamiliar word, look for _____**context clues**_____ near the word.

• • • MOTHER AND DAUGHTER • • •

Name _____

Read the paragraphs and complete the exercises.

A. Yollie asks her mother to wake her up when the movie is over.
When the film ends, however, Mrs. Moreno leaves Yollie asleep on
the couch. In good-humored revenge, Yollie sets up a glass of water
so her mother will spill it all over herself when the alarm rings. Then
she burns her mother's breakfast toast.

1. Complete the following generalization:

Yollie and her mother _____**often**_____ play jokes on each other.
(often, always, never)

2. Why did you choose the qualifying word you did?
The paragraph gives several examples of the jokes played between Yollie

and her mother, which would eliminate *never*. *Always* is an

overgeneralization, which leaves *often*.

B. Mrs. Moreno hopes her daughter will be a doctor. She buys Yollie
supplies and equipment to help her study. She saves money to pay for
Yollie's college education.
  Yollie's mother also encourages her daughter's social life. She dyes
a dress for her for a dance and buys her fancy new shoes to go with it.

1. What generalization can you make from the paragraphs you have just read?
Accept reasonable responses: Mrs. Moreno usually tries to help Yollie be

successful and happy.

2. What qualifying word, if any, did you use? Why?
Responses will vary.

SUMMARIZING
the **L**EARNING   A generalization is a single statement about _____**several**_____ events
or ideas. It tells about ___**events or ideas in general**___.

A MOTHER IN MANNVILLE

Name _____

A. Read each sentence. Underline the word or group of words that explains the boldface word.

1. The telling of this story is **belated,** but I have delayed because the story seems both simple and strange.

2. When we moved into our cabin in the woods, we were **impelled,** or forced, by the cold weather to hire someone to help us cut wood.

3. A man appeared—from nowhere, it seemed—and worked until the evening sky was **suffused** with color from the softly spreading light of the setting sun.

4. He was an open man and never used **subterfuge** to mislead us about how long he would stay.

5. Then, as the green leaves of summer turned into the fiery **vermilion** of autumn, he simply disappeared.

6. This behavior wasn't really **anomalous,** because his first appearance that beautiful evening had been just as irregular.

B. Use each of the boldface words in a sentence of your own. **Sentences will vary.**

1. _____

2. _____

3. _____

4. _____

5. _____

6. _____

A MOTHER IN MANNVILLE

Name _____

Complete the beginning-middle-ending chart to summarize "A Mother in Mannville." **Responses will vary.**

	PREDICTION	ACTUAL FEELINGS
Beginning	boy—lonely, angry woman—sympathetic	boy—cheerful, friendly woman—unfriendly
Middle	Responses will vary.	boy—eager, proud woman—sympathetic, closeness with boy
Ending	Responses will vary.	boy—sad woman—guilty, shocked about lie

••• A MOTHER IN MANNVILLE •••

Name _____

A. Use context clues and the definitions of the prefixes and suffixes in the box to choose the best definition of each underlined word.

> *un-* "not, opposite of" *re-* "back, again"
> *dis-* "opposite of, not" *-ly* "like or suited to"
> *-able* "being able to" *-ance* "act, state"
> *-less* "without" *-ed* "did or happened in the past"
> *-ful* "full of" *-ment* "action, result"
> *-ness* "state, quality"

1. The child had such unusual features that everyone who saw him found him <u>uncommonly</u> handsome.

   a. like ordinary

   b. not very often

   (c.) not like usual

   d. normally so

2. The passenger was fidgeting in <u>discomfort</u> due to the tightness of the seatbelt.

   a. being relaxed

   (b.) not at ease

   c. not funny

   d. full of pleasure

3. Johanna was completely confident in her ability to give her speech, thanks to her mother's constant <u>reassurance</u>.

   a. doubtful again

   (b.) encouraging again and again

   c. bad advice

   d. not confident at all

Name _____

4. The many shades of pink made a very <u>colorful</u> sunset.

    (a.) full of colors
    b. without colors
    c. opposite of color
    d. like colors

5. Our different views about the importance of education always result in <u>disagreements</u> between my mother and me.

    a. to have the same opinions
    (b.) opposite opinions
    c. to make unhappy
    d. results of similar views

6. Once a year the local banks auction items such as cars and houses that were <u>repossessed</u>, or taken back, because payments weren't made.

    a. the act of returning something
    b. the process of gaining items
    (c.) the process of getting back belongings
    d. the giving of gifts

B. Join suffixes and prefixes to other root words that you know, and use each new word in a sentence. Try to make four new words. **Sentences will vary.**

_____

_____

_____

_____

A MOTHER IN MANNVILLE

Name _____

Read the passage and complete the exercise.

A Night on the Mountain

Claude sat alone near the small campfire and replayed the argument in his mind. His older sister, Monica, thought Claude was a silly, fearful child, and had said so. Claude was determined to prove Monica wrong. With his parents' approval, he was going to stay out all night, camping by himself, about two miles from their ranch house. Then he would just watch the look on Monica's face as he strolled casually back into the house the next morning.

Claude noticed the dark coming on quickly. It can't be dusk yet, he thought, as he looked across the nearby lake. As the dark descended upon the campsite, Claude's imagination began to race. What kinds of wild animals lived in these woods? How would he protect himself from them? His heart began to pound. Could he run home in the dark?

Then he got hold of himself. He couldn't let Monica win this one. He decided to sleep his fears away.

Claude spread his sleeping bag inside his small pup tent. He was sure he'd feel a little safer within the thin walls of the tent. At first, listening to the howling wind and strange sounds, Claude huddled in his sleeping bag and hugged his pillow for comfort. But before he knew it, it was morning. The sounds outside the tent were no longer scary hoots and howls but happy bird songs.

Claude climbed out of the tent proudly. I wonder what Monica will think of me now, he thought. He was surprised to find that he no longer cared very much.

1. What internal conflicts does Claude face? **his need to prove himself to Monica and his fear**

2. What external conflicts does Claude face? **his sister and the dark, woodsy night**

3. What is the climax? **Claude thinks about running home at dark, but he gains control and stays the night.**

Name _____

Read the selection on these two pages, stopping after each section to complete the exercise that goes with it. Choose from the following strategies: reread, visualize, read on, refer to earlier section.

Accept reasonable responses. Possible answers are provided.

What strategy might help you to identify with what Rosa is feeling?

I could visualize. I could

imagine how a very hot,

dry day feels and

remember the smell of

wildflowers that I like.

This section suggests that Rosa had experienced danger sometime previously. Where could you look to see if the story will explain?

There is no explanation at

the beginning of the story,

so I would not reread. I

would have to read on, to

see if there is any more

information.

Rosa got out of her car and slowly walked to the side of the canyon. How she had missed her desert home. She loved going to college in the city, but the city did not smell or look or feel like the desert, which was fiercely hot and dry but, in the spring, full of wildflowers that grew nowhere else. Though it was no longer spring, she could smell them in her mind. She noted a sidewinder's track off to her right and wondered where the snake had gone underground to escape the heat.

Rosa started down the canyon path, checking the sky to be sure no rain was coming. It could fall suddenly and create raging rivers down hills that ordinarily were caked and dry. More than one desert hiker had been swept away in such a wash. As she descended into the canyon, she readjusted her backpack and, even though she planned to hike for only a couple of hours, checked to make sure her canteen was still watertight. She had repaired a leak in it just last week. An empty canteen could mean horrible thirst and even death in this country, as she knew only too well from her experience last summer.

The late afternoon sun poured down on Rosa's back as she hiked farther and farther into the canyon.

Name _____

When Rosa passed an outcropping, she heard a familiar warning sound. "Don't worry, sidewinder, my friend; the desert is more your home than mine," she said to herself as she gave the rocky place a wide berth.

After an hour, Rosa's canteen was half empty. She looked carefully for evidence of a pool or a small trickle of water to refill it. Again, images of last summer came back to haunt her. Tony had been almost dead by the time she found him, all because he planned to go for only a short walk and did not think he would need his canteen. Dying of thirst is not pleasant, and she remembered his dreamlike state, in which he did not know her but thought she was a gold miner. And she would never forget the sight of his parched skin and lips. She and Tony were closer than ever now, but she would always remember how close she came to losing her brother.

As Rosa started back up the canyon path, she was startled to see rain clouds overhead. She began to hurry, fearing she would not reach the top before the rain fell. But she climbed out of the canyon without incident just as the rain began. She hurried to the car, realizing that she could still surprise her family before dinner if she drove straight through.

A sidewinder is mentioned here, but you forget what it is. What can you do?

I can refer to the earlier section, where a sidewinder's track is mentioned. It is a kind of snake.

This seems important. The writer seems to be letting readers know how dangerous it is to travel in the desert without water. How could you be sure to remember this?

I could visualize and try to imagine how it feels to be very thirsty and not to know who anyone is.

This is a dangerous situation, but you forget why. What could you do?

Reread. She explains why sudden rainfalls can be dangerous earlier in the story.

• • • THE GREAT ANCESTOR HUNT • • •

Name _____

A. Complete the story by writing a word from the box on each line. Then underline the context clues that helped you choose your answers.

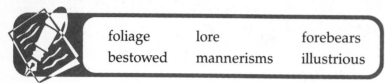

foliage	lore	forebears
bestowed	mannerisms	illustrious

Leroy asked his parents to tell him more about his grandmother,

grandfather, and his other ___**forebears**___ .

His mother told him that Leroy's grandfather had been famous, the

___**illustrious**___ mayor of a small town in Georgia. In fact,

she said, Leroy often reminded her of his grandfather because they

had the same ___**mannerisms**___ . She said they both gestured

when speaking.

The more Leroy learned about his grandfather, the more he felt that

his mother had ___**bestowed**___ a real compliment on him. And he

knew she did not grant compliments easily.

Leroy later put many of the stories and other ___**lore**___ about

his grandfather into a report on ancestors for his history class. As for his

grandfather's picture, it sits on Leroy's dresser among the

___**foliage**___ of several of Leroy's large leafy plants.

B. Write the word from the box on the line next to its definition.

1. ___**lore**___ facts, stories, and beliefs about a subject

2. ___**bestowed**___ given

3. ___**illustrious**___ distinguished

4. ___**mannerisms**___ special ways of speaking or doing things

5. ___**foliage**___ leaves of a plant

6. ___**forebears**___ ancestors

• • • THE GREAT ANCESTOR HUNT • • •

Name _____

Complete the K-W-L chart. **Responses will vary.**

K	W	L
What I Know	*What I Want to Know*	*What I Learned*
Ancestors are relatives from long ago.		

Name _____

Use structural analysis to figure out the meanings of the words below.
Read the meanings of the prefixes and suffixes in the box. Then read the
sentences and use context clues to determine the meaning of the boldface
word. Underline both the letter and the meaning you choose.

-ous "full of, having"	*-able* "capable of"	*re-* "again"
-ed "did or happened in the past"	*-s* "more than one"	*-ion* "result of"
un- "not"	*-ity* "condition or quality"	*-ure* "act or result of"
-logy "study of"		

1. Curtis gets the best grades in our class because he is very **studious.**
   (a) full of studying and learning   (b) tired of studying and learning
                    (c) smart and talented in school

2. Kayce was the maid of honor in the wedding when her mother **remarried.**
   (a) wed someone   (b) got wed again   (c) performed at a wedding

3. Because of her fascination with hereditary characteristics passed from one family
   generation to the next, Kerri decided to take a class in **genealogy.**
   (a) the study of life   (b) the study of movement
            (c) the study of heredity and family descent

4. When our last attempt at training her failed, we realized that our dog
   was just **uncontrollable.**
   (a) able to work well with others   (b) not able to be managed or restricted
              (c) willing to be trained

5. Snow in Florida, even in the winter, is a **rarity.**
   (a) condition of being rare or scarce   (b) quality of being common
              (c) result of rare drops in temperature

6. Tonia overcame her fear of **failure** when she ran for class president and won.
   (a) result of succeeding   (b) result of not succeeding   (c) being capable of succeeding

SUMMARIZING
the **L**EARNING   To figure out the _____**meaning**_____ of an unfamiliar word, break
                the word into its _____**parts**_____ .

Name _____

Read the selection and complete the exercise.

> The science of genetics studies heredity, or the passing on of traits from parents to children. Gregor Mendel, an Austrian monk, was one of the pioneers of genetics. Mendel worked with garden peas and discovered that each successive crop of this vegetable inherited specific traits, such as color, in a predictable way.
>
> Traits are passed from generation to generation through genes, or hereditary units. In human beings genes determine most physical characteristics, such as eye, skin, and hair color. Genes also determine blood type and the likelihood of getting certain diseases. Each organism inherits two sets of genes, one from each parent. Sometimes these gene pairs are identical. Other pairs carry different traits, one dominant and one recessive. A dominant trait is one that can be seen in the new organism, such as brown eyes. A recessive trait is one that is hidden in the organism but may show up in future generations if it is linked with another recessive gene of the same type.

1. If you write the summary for this selection, would you include a definition of heredity? Why or why not?
yes, because it is a main idea

2. Would you include a list of physical traits in your summary?
no, because these would be details

3. Would you include a statement about which organisms contain genes?
yes, because this is a main idea

4. Write your summary on another sheet of paper.
Summaries will vary but should include only the main ideas of the selection.

SUMMARIZING
the **L**EARNING

To write a summary, include the ____**main ideas**____ and leave out the ____**details**____.

Name _____

A. Read the sentences. Underline the correct meaning for the boldface word in each sentence.

1. Carla loved to visit her great-aunt's house, with its **pungent** smells of flavorful, healthful soups simmering on the stove.

  stale   <u>sharp</u>   rotten   sweet

2. Carla's Aunt Hilda was a home-care nurse whose desire to be a doctor had been **thwarted** by prejudice against professional women in her time.

  ignored   encouraged   <u>prevented</u>   laughed at

3. Hilda's patients usually loved her, and her presence in a house often helped lessen **dissension** among upset family members.

  snoring   overeating   singing   <u>quarreling</u>

4. She took care of her patients' **sustenance** as well as their medical needs.

  credits   <u>nourishment</u>   house   supplies and books

5. Occasionally one of her spoiled patients **berated** Hilda for some imagined slight, but she just ignored such incidents.

  <u>scolded</u>   forgot   reminded   praised

6. While patients sometimes tried to maintain bad habits, Hilda often found out, despite their **furtive** actions.

  <u>sneaky</u>   smeared   noisy   elaborate

7. Because Hilda paid **scrupulous** attention to her patients' needs and care, their health often improved.

  careless   religious   impatient   <u>careful</u>

B. Choose four of the boldface words, and use each in a sentence of your own. **Responses will vary.**

1. _____

2. _____

3. _____

4. _____

Name _____

Complete the prediction chart to summarize "Report from Part One."
Responses will vary.

	PREDICTIONS	ACTUAL MEMORIES
Parents and family life	singing smells and tastes	singing smells and tastes father's remedies
Memorable occasions	holidays	Christmas reading *Writer's Digest*

Name _____

A. Look at each pair of synonyms. Use the synonyms to complete the sentences. Then label each one *P* for *positive* or *N* for *negative* to indicate the connotation it carries.

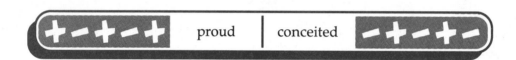

1. My father _____**chuckled**_____ as he read the comics page. __**P**__
2. Someone in the cafe _____**snickered**_____ when the dishes fell. __**N**__

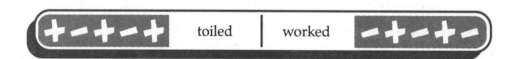

3. Sarah felt _____**proud**_____ that her science project had won. __**P**__
4. That _____**conceited**_____ cat acts as though humans were worthless. __**N**__

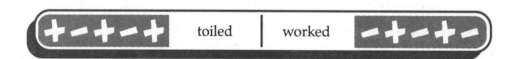

5. The employees at the steel mill _____**toiled**_____ near hot furnaces. __**N**__
6. My grandfather _____**worked**_____ on my broken guitar. __**P**__

B. Examine the thesaurus entry for the word *tiny*. Decide which words have a positive connotation, a negative connotation, or no connotation at all. Then, on another sheet of paper, write one sentence using a word for *tiny* that has a positive connotation and one sentence using a word with a negative connotation. **Sentences will vary.**

TINY: small, little, stunted, puny, petite, microscopic, runty, miniature

Name _____

Read the paragraphs and answer the questions.

> **O**n our street, everyone's family was normal except ours. This bothered me at first, but then I got used to it. What wonderful comic material my family would provide if ever I decided to go into show business!
>
> First, there was my grandfather, who lived mostly in the attic. That wasn't my parents' idea. Oh, no; it was his. He liked to be "above the trees" where he could set up his telescope. Of course, this "stargazing" got him into all kinds of trouble. He was always calling the police to report break-ins at the neighbors' houses. More often than not it was just someone coming home late or the family dog scratching at the front door.
>
> Then there was my uncle, who lived one floor down. He liked to invent things that no one could ever use. For instance, he invented a gadget for men to wear on their shoulders. It would tip their hats when they passed a lady. We tried in vain to tell him that people don't tip their hats anymore. He was convinced that the device would make him a million dollars. One day when I arrived at school, all the boys were standing there with hats on. "Good morning, Miss June," they drawled, and then they all tipped their hats. You think this embarrassed me? No way! I laughed! I thought it was great to have such a unique family.

1. What is the author's purpose in this passage?
   to entertain the reader with stories of her family

2. What is the author's viewpoint about her topic?
   She is proud of her unique family, and she thinks the stories will come in

   handy if she ever goes into show business.

SUMMARIZING
the **L**EARNING   An author's _____**purpose**_____ is the reason he or she has for
   writing. An author's _____**viewpoint**_____ consists of his or her
   opinions and attitudes.

••• REPORT FROM PART ONE •••

Name _____

Read the following passage. Think about the main idea or theme the writer is trying to communicate.

> **W**olfgang Amadeus Mozart was one of the world's greatest composers. Before he died, he wrote more than 600 musical works.
>
> Mozart's father was a respected musician and the leader of the orchestra in Salzburg, Austria. Mozart himself showed amazing musical talent at an early age. By the age of four, he could play the harpsichord, a musical instrument related to the piano. When he was five, he was composing music. Because his father realized that Mozart had a remarkable talent, he spent much of his time educating his son, both musically and academically. At a young age, Mozart started going with his father on concert tours of Europe, giving public performances.

1. Which of the following sentences best expresses the theme of this passage? Underline your choice.

   a. Mozart wrote more than 600 musical works.

   b. <u>Coming from a musical family and having been encouraged</u> <u>had a positive effect on Mozart's musical career.</u>

   c. Concert tours were popular in Mozart's time.

2. Why did you choose the sentence you did?
Answers will vary, but students should recognize that only sentence *b* puts the passage events into a broad statement. Sentence *a* merely states one fact from the passage, while sentence *c* makes a general statement that is not necessarily supported by the passage.

Name _____

Read the paragraphs and complete the exercise.

The Parkers packed hastily for their camping trip. As they drove out of town, Sandy said, "Mom, I don't think I turned off the air conditioner." Driving back to recheck the house, the family lost an hour on the road. Soon they were caught in a traffic jam. "Gosh, this is fun," exclaimed Larry. "I'd rather be doing my homework, frankly." Mr. Parker, who was driving, grumbled a reply.

When they reached the campground, all the sites with electrical hookups were occupied. "Well, we're supposed to be roughing it," sighed Mrs. Parker. "Get the food basket, will you, kids?"

"Uh, Mom, about the food basket," replied Sandy. "It looks a lot like the basket we keep the laundry in, doesn't it? Isn't that funny?"

Her mother stared at her in disbelief. "You don't mean . . . "

"Right," piped up Larry, "we're having socks and shirts for lunch. Which shall we barbecue first?"

1. Write a summary of the passage.

   Summaries will vary, but students should give the gist of the passage, not restate everything that happened.

2. Write a one-sentence generalization about the passage. Be prepared to explain your generalization.

   Accept reasonable responses: Poor planning can make an outing a nightmare.

Name _____

Read the following passage. Circle the context clues that helped you determine the meaning of each underlined word. Then write each word on the line next to its meaning.

"**W**e have discovered a formula that makes time travel possible," announced the (arrogant) scientists haughtily. The room fell silent. Reporters dropped their pens and pencils. One, who represented a well-known scientific journal, (hissed) irritably, "Did we come all the way over here to listen to science fiction?"

One scientist stood to the side, (rubbing his face.) His beard rasped his fingers. It had been a long day. Then he stepped forward.

"Here, I will show you the equation," he said. The room hushed as his chalk raced quickly over the chalkboard. Suddenly the atmosphere in the room was electric. The equation indeed showed that the probability of (accomplishing) time travel, so long doubted, was very high.

Now the reporters changed their tactics. (They were no longer skeptical and annoyed, but asked questions eagerly and complimented the scientists.)

1. _____**probability**_____ likelihood

2. _____**haughtily**_____ in a proud and scornful manner

3. _____**irritably**_____ in an impatient manner

4. _____**tactics**_____ methods, strategies

5. _____**rasped**_____ rubbed against something rough

WHAT ARE YOU GOING TO BE
WHEN YOU GROW UP?

Name _____

Fill in the story sequence chart to summarize "What Are You Going to Be When You Grow Up?"

THE CHARACTER'S PROBLEM
Mark feels confused because he hasn't chosen a career yet.

WHAT THE CHARACTER DOES TO SOLVE THE PROBLEM
FIRST, **Mark takes a trip fifteen years into his future; he discovers he is a mechanic but doesn't like this work.**

NEXT, **Mark concentrates on high-school football in order to become a professional athlete.**

FINALLY, **Mark takes a second time trip, discovers he could be a professional football player, but is dissatisfied with this career, too.**

THE CHARACTER'S SOLUTION
Mark decides to concentrate on the present, doing what he likes to do now.

Name _____

A. Read each sentence. Then write the two words from the sentence that are antonyms.

1. After the silence of the peaceful night, the cacophony caused by the motorcycle gang was unbearable.

silence, cacophony
_____

2. The carpenter walked around tapping the walls and listening for a hollow sound, but all he heard were thumps that told him the structure was solid.

hollow, solid
_____

3. The first time we stopped for help the person gave us vague directions, so we drove on until we found someone who was more clear.

vague, clear
_____

4. Every time the team made a crucial play, the bored sportscaster made it sound inconsequential.

crucial, inconsequential
_____

B. Use a word from the box to complete each analogy.

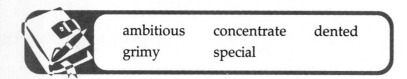

ambitious	concentrate	dented
grimy	special	

1. *High* is to *low* as *smooth* is to ___**dented**___.

2. *Top* is to *bottom* as *ordinary* is to ___**special**___.

3. *Rich* is to *poor* as *lazy* is to ___**ambitious**___.

4. *Night* is to *day* as *daydream* is to ___**concentrate**___.

5. *Tall* is to *short* as *clean* is to ___**grimy**___.

Name _____

A. Read the paragraph (here written in separate sentences) from "What Are You Going to Be When You Grow Up?" Look at the paraphrase of the first sentence below. Underline the words and phrases that have been used to paraphrase the sentence on the left. Then paraphrase the rest of the paragraph, sentence by sentence.
Students' paraphrases will vary.

ORIGINAL SENTENCE	PARAPHRASE
1. The chimpanzees <u>wore</u> yellow <u>uniforms</u> with long sleeves.	The chimpanzees <u>were dressed all alike</u> in yellow.
2. A man worked with them, showing them what to do.	
3. The chimpanzees could shovel dirt out of the hole very fast.	
4. They carried buckets of tar—far more than a man could.	

B. Now read the following paragraph, also taken from "What Are You Going to Be When You Grow Up?" Paraphrase the paragraph as a whole on the lines provided.

　　Somehow these chimpanzees looked different from the ones Mark had seen in the zoo. They tilted back their furry heads and listened when the man spoke to them. Could they understand English?
Students' paraphrases will vary.

_____

_____

· ·

SUMMARIZING *the* **L**EARNING

　　To paraphrase a sentence, a paragraph, or an idea means to **restate it in one's own words** _____.

...• WHAT ARE YOU GOING TO BE •...
WHEN YOU GROW UP?

Name _____

Read the passage and complete the exercise.

> **T**he Starship *Solar Wind* acknowledged the message and then
> went to warp speed. "Will we reach the stranded colonists in time,
> Dave?" asked the co-captain anxiously. "Their distress call said they
> had food and air for only another five days."
>
> "We'll make it," answered the captain grimly. He was concerned
> as a responsible Sky Armada officer, but he also had a brother in
> Delta Colony. The captain worked at the computer for several
> minutes and suddenly noticed that his hands were shaking and sweat
> was soaking his uniform. What would he tell his parents and sister if
> he did not reach Delta Colony in time to save his brother? Was he
> too emotionally involved to handle this mission? "Rita!" he snapped
> at his co-captain. "Take command of the ship. I'm going to check
> with engineering."

1. Which of the following gives the better summary of the passage?
   Explain your choice.

   a. A starship is enroute to rescue a group of space colonists. The
   captain's brother is in the colony, and the captain fears his judgment
   may be impaired by his emotional involvement.

   b. The captain of a starship is anxious because his brother is in
   trouble. His name is Dave. The captain tries to work at the
   computer and finds he is very nervous. He asks the co-captain
   to take over so he can check with engineering. The co-captain's
   name is Rita.

   The better choice is *a*; a summary should tell the basic story, not list

   specific details such as people's names.

2. Underline the statement that makes the best generalization about the
   passage. Be prepared to explain your choice.

   a. Space colonies should always be self-sufficient.
   b. Members of space fleets should never have feelings.
   c. One's job performance can often be affected by emotional stress.

• • • THE SEARCH FOR EARLY AMERICANS • • •

Name _____

Read the following paragraphs. Circle the context clues that helped you determine the meaning of each underlined word. Then write each word on the line next to its meaning.

H olly was chosen by her high school to work on a special summer archaeological dig. The scientists were working to excavate the remains of an ancient civilization. They hoped the various artifacts they uncovered would tell about the lives of the people who had lived there long ago.

Holly had no experience as an archaeologist, but she did not let this deter her or even slow her down. She was a hard worker and very interested in the history of ancient peoples.

At the site, Holly helped uncover shards of pottery and other clay objects. The pieces were to be put back together to give the archaeologists an idea of what the pottery had looked like.

Other workers dug up pendants for earrings and other jewelry. Necklaces were encrusted with precious stones. Some of the stones had fallen off, but many still clung to the jewelry's surface. Finally, some workers uncovered intricate mazes that the early people had constructed. The experts speculated that these complex passages were used to deceive and elude enemies. Holly felt she had never had such an exciting summer.

1. __**pendants**_____ ornaments that hang

2. __**deter**_____ to discourage from acting

3. __**encrusted**_____ covered with

4. __**artifacts**_____ tools, weapons, or other things made by people

5. __**shards**_____ fragments

6. __**intricate**_____ complicated

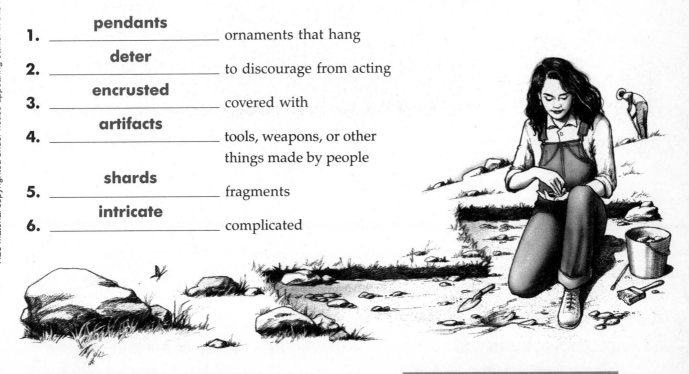

Name _____

Fill in the K-W-L chart to summarize "The Search for Early Americans."
Responses will vary.

K	W	L
What I Know	*What I Want to Know*	*What I Learned*
Archeologists study ruins and artifacts to learn about ancient civilizations.		

• • • THE SEARCH FOR EARLY AMERICANS • • •

Name _____

Read each sentence or short passage from "The Search for Early Americans," and notice the underlined words. Then complete the exercise.

1. "Over the next four years, Richard dug out nearly two hundred rooms in Pueblo Bonito. Soon he realized that <u>this pueblo</u> had been built differently than those at Mesa Verde. <u>There</u>, rooms were built as people moved in, . . .'"

To what does <u>this pueblo</u> refer? **Pueblo Bonito** _____

To what does <u>there</u> refer? **Mesa Verde** _____

2. "Some rooms were built of thin, flat rocks, <u>others</u> of large stones and mortar."

To what does <u>others</u> refer? **rooms** _____

3. "Richard found pottery and jewelry more beautiful than <u>any</u> <u>he</u> had ever seen."

To what does <u>any</u> refer? **pottery and jewelry** _____

To what does <u>he</u> refer? **Richard** _____

4. "High on the mesas north and west of Chaco were other ruins that looked similar. Could <u>they</u> have been part of Chaco?"

To what does <u>they</u> refer? **ruins on the mesas north and west of Chaco** _____

5. "Since the ancient ones had no written language, people are still searching for clues to <u>their</u> history."

To what does <u>their</u> refer? **ancient ones** _____

6. "Above all, Richard is remembered as one of the first Americans to prove that a great civilization existed in the desert long before Europeans settled <u>there</u>."

To what does <u>there</u> refer? **in the desert** _____

Name _____

Read the selection, and complete the exercises on these two pages.

Cahokia Mounds

Near today's city of St. Louis, Missouri, hundreds of miles east of Chaco Canyon, stand the remains of another early American civilization. It is called Cahokia.

One huge pyramid mound remains, as well as several smaller ones. Unfortunately, dozens of other mounds have been destroyed to make room for development.

1. Which statement in the two paragraphs is an opinion?
Unfortunately, dozens of other mounds have been destroyed to make room

for development.

2. What bias do you think the author expresses here? __**Accept reasonable responses:**__
Ancient ruins should be left intact.

The large pyramid is called Monks' Mound because French monks lived there and grew vegetables and trees on it in the nineteenth century. This mound is the largest earthen pyramid in North America. Certainly it is the most interesting.

3. The words *largest* and *most interesting* in the paragraph are both descriptions. Which refers to a fact, and which refers to an opinion? Explain your answer.
Largest **refers to a fact because size can be proven or verified.** *Most*

interesting **refers to an opinion because interest can be neither proven**

nor verified.

The Cahokians had neither beasts of burden nor wagons. So the large mound, consisting of over 22 million cubic feet of earth, was constructed a basketful of earth at a time. Cahokian mounds are hard to preserve because of their earthen content. They erode easily. The mounds are not as attractive as the distinctively shaped stone pyramids built by other Indian cultures. The Cahokian mounds look more like ordinary small hills and are easily overlooked because of this characteristic.

Name _____

4. Which statement in the paragraph is an opinion?

The mounds are not as attractive as the distinctively shaped stone pyramids

built by other Indian cultures.

5. What bias do you think the author expresses here?

Accept reasonable responses: a preference for stone pyramids

      Archaeologists are in the process of excavating the Cahokian
civilization and so far have uncovered only about one percent of the site.
This partial excavation is enough to tell them that the city of Cahokia was
the largest North American city through the eighteenth century. It
reached its peak between 1000 and 1200 A.D. while Europe slept through
the Dark Ages. At that time, Cahokia was larger than London.

6. What is the opinion stated above?

Europe slept through the Dark Ages.

7. What bias do you think the author expresses here? **Accept reasonable responses:**

Little of interest occurred in Europe during the Dark Ages.

      What happened to these early Americans? Scientists are still
searching for answers. Overpopulation has been suggested, resulting in
loss of resources and food. Climate change affecting the growing season is
also a possibility. If you become an archaeologist, perhaps you will find
the answer.

8. Use facts from the selection to write a brief summary.

Summaries will vary, but students should use a minimum of five facts from

the selection.

HBJ material copyrighted under notice appearing earlier in this work.

SUMMARIZING
the **L**EARNING

Facts are statements about things that ____**actually**____

____**happened**____ . Opinions are statements of

____**belief**____, ____**judgment**____ , or ____**feeling**____ .

Name _____

Read the nonfiction passages on these two pages, and answer the questions. Then write the strategy or strategies you used to answer each question. **Accept reasonable responses. Possible answers are provided.**

> **Strategies**
>
> preview/survey   predict   summarize
>
> use prior knowledge   self-question

From Politics to Sports

Many common elements in our daily lives are easily taken for granted—ideas such as democracy and team sports, for example. But where did these things come from? Are they as homegrown "American" as we think?

1. What do you think this selection will be about? Why?

It will be about the true origins of ordinary "American" things, such as

democracy and team sports. The title and the paragraph suggest this

content. (preview, predict)

2. What are two questions you might ask from the reading you have done so far?

Where did our political ideas come from? Where did our popular sports come

from? (self-question)

Actually, these things—both political ideas and team sports—*are* American in a sense. That is, they were practiced or played by people who lived in North or South America long before Europeans and others came to these shores. The idea of democracy, for example, was found in the political structure of the Iroquois, Native Americans living in northeastern North America.

As for team sports, the Mayans of Central America played one centuries ago. In their difficult game, players used only knees or hips to try to hit a rubber ball through a vertical stone ring high on a wall. The Spanish observed the game and took the idea of team sports back to Europe.

Name _____

3. What questions does this part of the selection answer?

where the idea of democracy came from and where team sports came from

(summarize)

4. What idea or ideas have you learned that surprise you?

Responses will vary. (summarize)

The foods grown by the Indians of the Americas helped change the eating habits of the world. Potatoes, literally hundreds of varieties, were grown by the Incas and other people of South America. A cheap source of nutrition and high in vitamin C, the potato was taken back to Europe by the Spanish and transformed the diet of Europeans. Other vegetables and fruits raised by Native Americans, such as tomatoes and corn, are a regular part of our diet today.

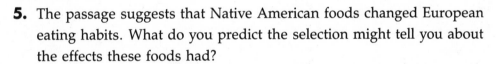

5. The passage suggests that Native American foods changed European eating habits. What do you predict the selection might tell you about the effects these foods had?

The selection says the potato is nutritious and high in vitamin C, which

means it is healthful. I know that fruits and vegetables in general are

necessary for a healthful diet. I predict that later in the selection I will read

that eating the Native American foods made Europeans healthier. (use prior

knowledge, predict)

6. Summarize in a paragraph the passages you have read.

Responses will vary but should include the main idea that many common

elements of today's world came from Native Americans. (summarize)

••• TOUCHMARK •••

Name _____

Complete the story below by writing a word from the box in each blank space.
Then write the letter for the correct definition on the line before each word.

c	1. demurely	a. courageous
f	2. enthralled	b. real or imagined wrong
g	3. foray	c. modestly, shyly
b	4. grievance	d. lazy
h	5. outlandish	e. move in a sneaky way
d	6. shiftless	f. spellbound, fascinated
e	7. skulk	g. raid or expedition
a	8. stalwart	h. strange or unfamiliar

It was the night of the big event. Mr. Potter's class was performing an original play about the daring __foray__ that went down in history as the Boston Tea Party and the __stalwart__ colonists who bravely took up the cause of liberty.

A prologue, read __demurely__ by one of the shyest girls in the class, explained the __grievance__ that the colonists had against the British. Once the actors strode onto stage in their __outlandish__ costumes and bizarre makeup, the audience was and __enthralled__ did not make a sound. The only flaw in the whole play was caused by a __shiftless__ boy who had not learned his lines and began to __skulk__ off of the stage. Nevertheless, the audience gave the performance a standing ovation.

••• TOUCHMARK •••

Name _____

Complete the character traits chart to summarize "Touchmark." **Responses will vary.**

CHARACTER	SPECIAL TRAITS	CONFLICTS FACED
Nabby	**curious, bold, witty, honorable**	**conflicts with her society's restrictions on women's roles; conflict with Master Butler over her presence at the Tea Party; conflict within herself about whether to reveal Lonzo's theft**
Emily	**gentle, kind, artistic**	**conflict within herself about whether she should help Nabby break her father's command**
Tobias Butler	**stern, brave, unsympathetic**	**conflict with the British; conflict with Nabby about her disobedience**
Lonzo	**shiftless, dishonest**	**conflict with Nabby about mending his coat, wondering if his theft will be discovered**

Name _____

A. Use each pair of homophones below to complete the sentences.

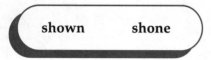

shown   shone

1. Had the moon ___shone___ brightly that night, the patriots might have been discovered.

2. If Nabby had ___shown___ her face at the harbor, Master Butler would have been furious.

aught   ought

3. Emily told Nabby she ___ought___ to obey Master Butler.

4. Nabby wondered if Master Butler would have ___aught___ to say about the previous night's events.

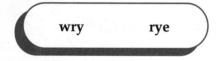

wry   rye

5. Nabby suspected that Lonzo had also been skulking around the previous night, so she gave him a ___wry___ smile.

6. The family's breakfast consisted of a hot drink made from chicory root, ___rye___ bread, homemade jam, and potted herring.

B. Study the pronunciations of the homographs below. Then read the sentences, and decide which pronunciation fits the underlined word. Write the letter in the blank.

close: **a.** klōz   **b.** klōs

1. Had the tree not been so <u>close</u> to the house, Nabby could not have climbed down it. ___b___

2. Emily got up to <u>close</u> the window after her. ___a___

rebel: **a.** reb'əl   **b.** ri·bel'

3. A Patriot in the American Revolution was considered to be a <u>rebel</u> by the British. ___a___

4. Nabby seemed the type to <u>rebel</u> against injustice. ___b___

Name _____

Read the description of each book. Then identify the book as one of
the literary forms listed in the box.

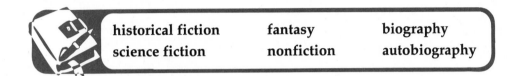

| historical fiction | fantasy | biography |
| science fiction | nonfiction | autobiography |

1. a book in which a fictional character takes part in the Boston

   Tea Party __historical fiction__

2. a collection of eyewitness accounts of events leading up to the

   Revolutionary War ___nonfiction___

3. the story of the Boston Tea Party as told by a fictional boy serving on

   one of the three British East India Company ships __historical fiction__

4. a story in which George Washington travels to the twenty-third century

   to convince leaders on Earth that they should give a colony planet its

   independence ___science fiction___

5. a story in which George Washington appears to a young boy in

   a dream and helps him learn about history ___fantasy___

6. the true story, written by somebody else, of a servant in the home

   of a famous Boston patriot ___biography___

7. a book about the life of George Washington, written by

   himself ___autobiography___

SUMMARIZING
the **L**EARNING   Historical fiction combines ___real___ settings,

characters, and events with ___fictional___ characters and events.

••• TOUCHMARK •••

Name _____

Imagine that while Nabby is down at Boston Harbor, Emily writes the following entry in her diary. Read it and answer the questions.

December 16, 1773

    Oh, Dear Diary, I am so worried about Nabby. It's true she didn't cross the threshold tonight, which Father forbade us to do, but she is clearly disobeying! If Nabby gets a reputation for deception, people will not respect her, and what is a woman without respect? Nabby has stuffed cushions beneath her bedclothes and climbed out the window, down a tree, into the street. I worry not only for her honor, but for her safety.

    On the other hand, perhaps Nabby was right to venture forth tonight. Nabby is as stalwart as any of the lads helping our cause, and it seems unfair for her to be excluded from the excitement and opportunities only because she is a woman. Perhaps she is helping the Patriot cause tonight, and if she does guard herself well, she will have such stories to tell! Sometimes I do wonder if she puts herself at peril so I can share in her adventures, for she did say exciting stories would give me ideas for my sketches.

1. What two ideas are compared and contrasted in Emily's diary entry?
Accept reasonable responses: that Nabby was wrong to leave

the house and that she was right to help her cause.

2. What phrase divides the two points of view? **On the other hand**

3. What are two good reasons why Nabby should not have done what she did? **Accept**
reasonable responses. Nabby's behavior was disobedient and amounted to

deception. Her behavior put her in danger.

4. What are two reasons why Nabby did what she did? **Accept reasonable responses.**

It allowed her to claim her rightful place among the Patriots. It was likely to bring

excitement into Emily's sheltered life.

HBJ material copyrighted under notice appearing earlier in this work.

74   **Comparing-Contrasting/ Making Judgments**   Practice Book ▪ **VOICES AND REFLECTIONS**

Name _____

A. Assume, now, that you are Emily, and it is the following day. You have come to some conclusions about Nabby's behavior the previous evening. Although you may not have the courage to state these ideas before your parents or Nabby, you write them in your diary. Write an entry in which you make judgments about Nabby's behavior. Begin your entry with one of the following sentences.

> I think that Nabby was wrong to do what she did.
> I am happy that Nabby did what she did.

Answers will vary.

_____

_____

_____

_____

_____

B. Answer the questions below.

1. Having read Emily's diary entry on page 74, what judgment can you make about a woman's place in colonial society? **Accept reasonable responses. Women in colonial society were unfairly excluded from political struggles because of their gender. They were expected to be obedient and honest.**

2. Has a woman's place in society changed? If so, how? **Accept reasonable responses. Women can take part directly in political struggles. Honesty is still valued, but cooperation with the opposite sex has replaced obedience in most circles.**

Name _____

A. Complete the story by writing a word from the box on each line.

> **a.** dexterity   **b.** languished   **c.** proceeds   **d.** relented
> **e.** tacking   **f.** tentative   **g.** single-handedly

The *Blue Fin* was a private fishing vessel until the outbreak of the Revolutionary War. Its crewmembers wished for little more from life than to fish the Atlantic seawaters and use the

proceeds from their catch to support their families. When heavy winds damaged a sail or net, a crewmember would

make repairs **single-handedly**. Such repairs required

dexterity and strength, but the crew enjoyed the feeling of self-sufficiency.

With the outbreak of the war, the captain was issued a "letter of marque" allowing his ship to engage British vessels in battle as a privateer. From the beginning, the support of the crew

was **tentative**. Many had sympathy for the colonists' cause, but they had not signed onto the *Blue Fin* to fight. After several

half-hearted battles, many injured crewmembers **languished** in the ship's hold. There was little hope that they would see their families soon. Finally, one bleak afternoon, as the *Blue Fin* was

tacking back to shore after suffering many losses, the

captain **relented**. The *Blue Fin* would no longer be a privateer.

B. Write the correct letter on the line before each definition.

____ **a** **1.** skill in using the hands or body

____ **d** **2.** became more compassionate or less severe

____ **e** **3.** maneuvering a ship against the wind by a series of zigzag turns

____ **b** **4.** weakened from restless longing

____ **c** **5.** profit obtained

____ **g** **6.** without assistance

____ **f** **7.** not firm; subject to change

••• JAMES FORTEN •••

Name _____

Fill in the **K-W-L** chart to summarize "James Forten." Accept reasonable responses.

K *What I Know*	W *What I Want to Know*	L *What I Learned*
James Forten grew up in Philadelphia. He fought in the Revolutionary War.	What battles did he take part in? What happened to him in these battles? What did James Forten do after the war was over? Why is Forten remembered today?	Forten was a sailor on the *Royal Louis*, a privateer; he helped defeat the *Active*. He was taken prisoner by the British and put on a prison ship. He became a very successful businessman. He was a significant African American contributor to the colonies' battle for independence; he worked for the abolition of slavery.

••• JAMES FORTEN •••

Name _____

Use the partial table of contents and index to answer the questions. If you answer a question with a page number or numbers, also identify the book part you used.

THE AMERICAN REVOLUTION

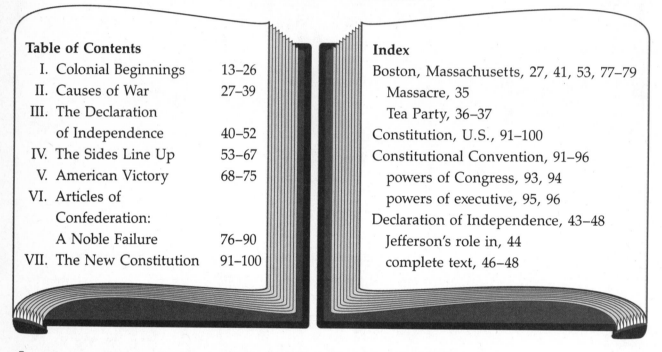

Table of Contents

I. Colonial Beginnings   13–26
II. Causes of War   27–39
III. The Declaration
     of Independence   40–52
IV. The Sides Line Up   53–67
V. American Victory   68–75
VI. Articles of
    Confederation:
    A Noble Failure   76–90
VII. The New Constitution   91–100

Index

Boston, Massachusetts, 27, 41, 53, 77–79
    Massacre, 35
    Tea Party, 36–37
Constitution, U.S., 91–100
Constitutional Convention, 91–96
    powers of Congress, 93, 94
    powers of executive, 95, 96
Declaration of Independence, 43–48
    Jefferson's role in, 44
    complete text, 46–48

1. Where would you look to read the actual words of the Declaration of Independence? **pages 46–48; index**

2. Where would you be likely to find information on King George III? **pages 27–39; table of contents**

3. Where would you look to see which came first, the Boston Massacre or the Boston Tea Party? **pages 35, 36–37; index**

4. Where would you be likely to find the names of George Washington's generals as well as the British military leaders? **pages 53–67; table of contents**

5. Where could you find a list of the duties and responsibilities of Congress and the executive branch? **pages 93, 94, 95, 96; index**

6. Where would you be likely to find reasons for the need for a new Constitution? **pages 76–90; table of contents**

Name _____

Explain how you would find the information requested in each item,
using either the card catalog or the computer data base in your library.

1. You enjoyed reading a book on the Civil War by the author Bill Smith.
How can you find out whether he has written books on the
Revolutionary War period?

Look in the card catalog under *Smith, Bill* for titles of books he has written.

Enter *Smith, Bill—author* in the computer.

2. You want to see how many books your library has on Crispus Attucks.
What do you do?

Look in the card catalog under *Forten, James—subject*. Make a list of titles.

Enter *Forten, James—subject* in the computer. Make a list of titles held by

your library branch.

3. You want specific information on the Boston Massacre and the Boston
Tea Party. Would you enter *American Revolution—subject* in the data base?
Why or why not?

No. This would give you dozens of titles, without telling you which books

covered the topics best. Enter *Boston Massacre—subject* and *Boston Tea*

***Party—subject* in the data base to limit the number of titles.**

4. You are looking for a specific book—*Pre-Revolutionary America* by
Barbara Brown. You enter *Brown, Barbara—author* into the data base. The
screen tells you there are three Barbara Browns who write books. Since
you do not know which one she is, what do you do next?

Enter *Pre-Revolutionary America—title* into the computer.

• • • WE HOLD THESE TRUTHS • • •

Name _____

A. Read each sentence. Underline the word or words that explain the
boldface word.

1. The American colonists believed that certain rights were **unalienable,**
   that they could be neither given nor taken away.

2. Their **prudence,** or good judgment, led them to write down their
   grievances against King George III in the Declaration of
   Independence.

3. The world had a right to know of the violations of freedom and
   infringements of their rights imposed by the British.

4. Even today the record of British injustice to the colonies **evinces** the
   British plan for domination, while the colonies' own document
   demonstrates their resistance to this behavior.

5. The king's **despotism,** or tyranny, was one of the colonists' major
   complaints.

6. In addition, they expressed many **censures** of the British soldiers,
   criticizing the soldiers' ill treatment of colonists.

7. The colonists hoped that a listing of wrongs would convince readers
   of the **rectitude** of their position, its essential rightness.

8. The abuses had been going on long enough to convince the colonists
   that they were not of a **transient** nature and would not pass quickly.

9. They wished to be **absolved** of all further allegiance to the British
   crown and released from further taxation.

10. **Invariably,** many rulers misunderstood the Declaration, as tyrants will
    always fail to understand those who wish to be free.

B. On another sheet of paper, use the words *prudence, invariably,*
unalienable, and *transient* in your own sentences.
Responses will vary.

• • • WE HOLD THESE TRUTHS • • •

Name _____

Complete the K-W-L chart to summarize "We Hold These Truths."

Responses will vary.

K	W	L
What I Know	*What I Want to Know*	*What I Learned*
The Declaration of Independence declared America's freedom from Britain.		

•••WE HOLD THESE TRUTHS•••

Name _____

Each pair of sentences states the same information with either a positive or a negative connotation. Read each sentence. Write *P* after the sentence with the positive view and *N* after the sentence with a negative view. Then write the two words, one from each sentence, that do the most to give the positive or negative slant.

1. a. The colonists stood in opposition to the policies of King George III.

P
_____

b. The Americans chose insubordination instead of loyalty to the

British Crown. ____**N**____

opposition, insubordination
_____

2. a. After they had bickered for weeks, the representatives finally reached

an agreement. ____**N**____

b. When the body of lawmakers had debated for a period of time, they

came to an understanding. ____**P**____

bickered, debated
_____

3. a. Jefferson's thinking was all first-rate, but his public behavior

was forbidding. ____**N**____

b. Jefferson's reserved demeanor concealed a brilliant mind.

P
_____

forbidding, reserved
_____

4. a. An enthusiastic throng gathered to hear the reading of the new

Declaration of Independence. ____**P**____

b. The newly signed Declaration of Independence was read to the

noisy rabble. ____**N**____

throng, rabble
_____

Connotation and Denotation/ Slanted Writing   Practice Book ▪ **VOICES AND REFLECTIONS**

••• WE HOLD THESE TRUTHS •••

Name _____

A. Read the paragraph to find the stated main idea and supporting details.

The Declaration of Independence was set in motion by both enemies and friends of the American colonists. In 1795 the Continental Congress attempted a reconciliation with King George III. He responded by calling the colonists rebels and cutting off their trade with England. Shortly afterward Thomas Paine published his pamphlet *Common Sense*, which helped Americans see that they owed no allegiance to the king or to England. The Declaration was issued several months after the actions of King George and Paine.

1. What is the stated main idea of the paragraph?

The Declaration of Independence was set in motion by both enemies and

friends of the American colonists.

2. What are the supporting details?

Accept reasonable responses; students should include a restatement of the

actions of both King George and Thomas Paine.

B. Read the paragraph from the Declaration of Independence. Write the implied main idea on the lines.

"In every stage of these Oppressions We have petitioned for Redress in the most humble terms: Our repeated Petitions have been answered only by repeated injury. A Prince [King George III], whose character is thus marked by every act which may define a Tyrant, is unfit to be the ruler of a free people."

Accept reasonable responses; students should recognize that the major

thrust of the paragraph is that King George is largely responsible for the

colonists' desire for independence.

SUMMARIZING the LEARNING

The central thought or gist of a paragraph is the ___**main**___ ___**idea**___. The ___**details**___ provide the specific information and support the main idea.

• • • WE HOLD THESE TRUTHS • • •

Name _____

Read the paragraphs and answer the questions.
Accept reasonable responses. Possible answers are provided.

The most persuasive voice for American independence belonged not to an American but to a British subject. Thomas Paine came to the colonies from England in 1774. An enemy of monarchy and of King George III, Paine wrote a pamphlet called *Common Sense*. In it he presented to the colonists arguments for independence. George Washington said that *Common Sense* contained "unanswerable reasoning." It was undoubtedly the chief cause of his decision to support American independence.

1. List two facts you read. **Thomas Paine came to America in 1774; he wrote** **Common Sense, which presented arguments for colonial independence.**

2. List one opinion you read in the paragraph. **Thomas Paine was the most** **persuasive voice for American independence.**

3. What is the author's viewpoint in this paragraph? **The British Thomas Paine was a** **more important voice for American independence than any American voice.**

Thomas Jefferson is considered to be America's chief Revolutionary hero. His political ideas in the Declaration laid the foundation for the new nation. Besides this accomplishment, he was an architect, a lawyer, an amateur musician and naturalist, and an inventor. Later Thomas Jefferson served as President of the United States.

4. List two facts you read in the paragraph. **Thomas Jefferson's political ideas laid a** **foundation for the new nation; he was President of the United States.**

5. List one opinion you read. **Jefferson is considered to be America's chief** **Revolutionary hero.**

6. What is the author's purpose? **to inform readers about Thomas Jefferson**

7. What is the author's viewpoint? **Thomas Jefferson was a remarkable man.**

Fact-Opinion/Author's Purpose-Viewpoint   Practice Book ■ **VOICES AND REFLECTIONS**

• • • WE HOLD THESE TRUTHS • • •

Name _____

A. Read each part of the Declaration of Independence and the
paraphrase that follows it. Then answer the questions.

> "He has called together legislative bodies at places unusual,
> uncomfortable, and distant from the depository of their public Records, for
> the sole purpose of fatiguing them into compliance with his measures."
>
> He has scheduled meetings far from legislators' offices in order to make
> them so tired that they will agree to whatever he wants.

1. Is this a good paraphrase of the statement? __yes_____

2. Why or why not? __It restates the main idea in different words._____

> "He has affected to render the Military independent of, and superior to,
> the Civil power."
>
> He supports the military in all matters.

3. Is this a good paraphrase of the statement? __no_____

4. Why or why not? __It is too general and does not include all the relevant__
__information.__

B. Read each statement from the Declaration, and write your own paraphrase.

1. "He has dissolved Representative Houses repeatedly, for opposing
with manly firmness his invasions on the rights of the people."
Accept reasonable responses: He has disbanded governing bodies that
__object to his removing people's rights.__

2. "He has plundered our seas, ravaged our Coast, burnt our towns, and
destroyed the lives of our people."
Accept reasonable responses: He wrecked sea trade, invaded the country,
__set fire to towns, and ruined people's lives.__

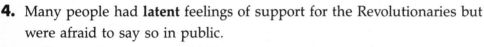

•••1787•••

Name _____

Read the sentences. Underline the correct meaning for the boldface word in each sentence.

1. The printer worked slowly and **meticulously** to prepare the long document.

    angrily   <u>carefully</u>   hopelessly   greedily

2. When the document had been brought in, the **stipulation** had been that it would be ready by the end of the week.

    <u>condition</u>   argument   misunderstanding   question

3. The printer **surmised,** though he had no proof, that this was the famous document he had heard so much about recently.

    doubted   feared   resented   <u>guessed</u>

4. Many people had **latent** feelings of support for the Revolutionaries but were afraid to say so in public.

    disgusted   open   <u>hidden</u>   no

5. The printer hoped to make a perfect copy, but after all, he had not been given the gift of **infallibility.**

    <u>freedom from error</u>   hope   freedom from fear   trustworthiness

6. He was tired, and try as he might, he feared that **inevitably** he would make a mistake at some point.

    happily   unrelentingly   unruly   <u>certainly</u>

7. However, when he finally showed the document to his family, they said with **unanimity** that it was perfect.

    <u>complete agreement</u>   complete disagreement   confidence   lack of confidence

8. Proudly, the printer **affixed** his seal to the document and awaited those who would come to claim it for history.

    took off   hid carefully   covered up   <u>attached</u>

• • • 1787 • • •

Name _____

Complete the fact-fiction chart to summarize "1787."
Accept reasonable responses.

HISTORICAL FACTS	FICTIONAL DETAILS
the Constitutional Convention	Jared Mifflin
reading the Preamble	Jared's thoughts and emotions
George Washington	Hetty
Benjamin Franklin	William
Henry Blair	

Name _____

Read each passage, and identify the point of view as first person, third-person limited, or third-person omniscient. Then tell why you chose that point of view.

1.   The tension around the dinner table was strong. The family all knew that the new Constitution was being signed in the state capitol that day. The head of the family, Frederick Miller, had worked hard to defeat the document and felt his failure keenly. His son Jason, who favored the document but feared his father, kept his silence.

Veronica Miller, Frederick's wife, favored the Constitution and made no secret of it. "We will all rest better knowing that the workings of our new nation will spring from principles that have been so thoroughly discussed," she said quietly, but effectively. "Now, let us give thanks and eat."

Third-person omniscient: The writer knows everyone's thoughts

and feelings.

2.   William, the capitol aide, rushed here and there, delivering notes from one representative to another. *This is certainly a more exciting job than working on the farm,* he thought to himself. *I wish I knew what they're going to say to the reporters and what they really think. It's hard to tell because they are always so polite when they speak.* Suddenly the doorbell rang, and William rushed to admit a group of reporters.

Third-person limited: It is told from one character's point of view, and he

cannot see into other people's minds.

3.   I write this column on an historic day. The Constitution of the United States will be formally signed today by our state legislators. As a journalist, I should remain noncommittal, but it is hard not to be proud of what has been accomplished. I will be able to tell my children that I was there on the day our state joined the new Union.

First-person point of view: It is told by an "I" character.

• • • 1787 • • •

Name _____

Read the passage and answer the questions.

Accept reasonable responses. Possible answers are provided.

The framers of the Constitution for the new American republic were guided by their experiences as British subjects. They constructed a three-branched government—executive, legislative, and judicial. American colonists would never have wanted a strong chief executive to remind them of the British king.

The framers set up a two-chambered congress. Its members, who represented different parts of the population, would make laws and impose taxes. This form of congress was far superior to the English Parliament.

The chief claim to fame for the framers of the Constitution is the Bill of Rights. The First Amendment guarantees individual rights in areas such as freedom of speech, press, religion, and assembly, and it protects individuals arrested for a crime.

Many people consider the United States Constitution an ideal document. However, while it has much to recommend it, Americans should not forget that the original document upheld slavery and ignored the rights of Native Americans. It also did not recognize the rights of women. The original Constitution was a document both politically brilliant and flawed.

1. List two facts you read. **The framers of the U.S. Constitution were guided by their experiences as British subjects. They set up a three-branched government and a two-chambered legislature.**

2. List two opinions you read. **American colonists would never have wanted a strong chief executive to remind them of the British king. Congress was superior to the English Parliament.**

3. What is the author's purpose? **to inform readers of unique and positive points about the original Constitution, but also to acknowledge its flaws**

4. What is the author's viewpoint in the passage? **The original U.S. Constitution is worthy of respect, but its flaws make it less than an ideal document.**

Name _____

Read each numbered item of information. Then write in which of the following reference sources the information would most likely be found: dictionary, thesaurus, encyclopedia, atlas, almanac, *Books in Print, Readers' Guide to Periodical Literature*, computer data base. Some items may be found in more than one source.

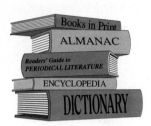

1. the etymologies of the words *monarchy, aristocracy,* and *anarchy*
   dictionary
   _____

2. a map of pre-Revolutionary War America
   atlas, encyclopedia
   _____

3. titles of books by Milton Meltzer
   ***Books in Print,* computer data base**
   _____

4. the current number of legislative representatives of each state
   almanac, current encyclopedia
   _____

5. synonyms and antonyms for the words *freedom* and *resistance*
   thesaurus, dictionary
   _____

6. magazine articles about celebrations of the American bicentennial
   Readers' Guide to Periodical Literature
   _____

7. historical data about the kings and queens of England
   encyclopedia
   _____

8. biographies of Thomas Paine and Abigail Adams
   ***Books in Print,* computer data base**
   _____

9. distances between major cities in the United States
   atlas, encyclopedia
   _____

10. list of United States Presidents and Vice Presidents to the present time
    encyclopedia, almanac
    _____

Name _____

Read the following paragraphs. Circle the context clues that help you determine the meaning of each underlined word. Then write each word on the line next to its meaning.

The dragons came from miles around to gather in a clearing. One (self-important) dragon who was trying to speak (frowned) and announced huffily, "Settle down, now; settle down. It's time we got started. You, over there, close your mouths; you're toasting the trees!"

"Oh, come now, Megath," crooned his sister, (trying to calm) him. Megath smiled at her and relented. He spoke in a more normal tone of voice. "Humans have been seen in the kingdom again," he stated. "We must decide what to do."

"We must stay hidden," replied one (very large old) dragon, who spoke in a (slow) and ponderous voice. "If they see us, they will declare war."

"Then let's declare war first," said a young female warrior, who had a (red lightning streak) emblazoned on her dragon (cape.)

"Could we have just a smidgeon of sense in this discussion?" demanded a male dragon. "I know it's asking a lot, but just a (small bit) of sense would tell us that secrecy is the best policy until we know what the humans are up to."

After much discussion, they agreed. Then they took off, flying upward through the air in (large circles,) creating one huge gyre that shadowed all the trees.

1. _____**emblazoned**_____ placed as a bright decoration

2. _____**gyre**_____ spiraling circle

3. _____**huffily**_____ in an offended way

4. _____**crooned**_____ murmured in a soothing tone

5. _____**ponderous**_____ large and heavy

6. _____**smidgeon**_____ tiny piece

GREAT-GRANDFATHER
DRAGON'S TALE

Name _____

Complete the story chart to summarize "Great-Grandfather Dragon's
Tale." **Accept reasonable responses. Possible answers are provided.**

What I know from the beginning . . .
**The dragons live in a cave. Dragons celebrate Thanksgiving but
haven't always. Characters include an old dragon, a mother
dragon, and five little dragons. Characters and setting are fantasy.**

What I learned later . . .
**Dragons once ruled the earth but were overthrown by humans. The
old dragon who tells the story explains that dragons nearly became
extinct hundreds of years ago.**

I predict that . . .
The dragons will meet a human, and they will become friends.

What really happened . . .
**One human, Georgi, became friendly with the dragons, and the
dragons and humans made peace.**

Name _____

Read each example of figurative language. Identify it as a simile, a metaphor, or an example of personification. Then tell what two things are being compared in each example.

1. The tree scratched on the windowpanes with jagged fingernails.

personification   the tree and a person with jagged fingernails

2. Tomita's grief made her heart a block of ice.

metaphor   a heart and a block of ice

3. As we approached, a large dog ran yelping from behind the house and stood at attention on the front stoop.

personification   a dog and a soldier

4. After my sneezing fit, my throat was as rough as sandpaper.

simile   a throat and sandpaper

5. Thunder galloped across the sky and seemed to pull up short just above my house.

metaphor   thunder and a galloping horse

6. I thought about who the thief might be, and suddenly a dreadful idea lodged in my mind as if it meant to stay awhile.

personification   an idea and an uninvited or unwelcome visitor

7. The chattering birds sounded like small children at a water fountain.

simile   birds and small children at a water fountain

SUMMARIZING the LEARNING   A _____simile_____ compares two unlike things, using *like* or *as*. _____Personification_____ gives _____human_____ qualities to ideas, objects, or animals. A _____metaphor_____ compares two unlike things without using *like* or *as*.

Name _____

Each group of sentences features words made up of a Latin root and prefixes and suffixes. Decide which word fits the definition in the parentheses, and circle it. Use a dictionary to find the meanings of the prefixes and suffixes you do not know.

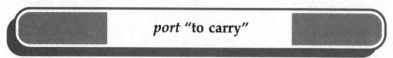
port "to carry"

1. Is your typewriter (able to be carried)?

portage (portable) important

2. The (one who carries back news) called you today about the robbery.

(reporter) reporting exportable

3. My uncle owns an (something carried in) store.

expert export (import)

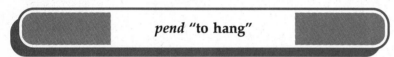
pend "to hang"

4. We fearfully awaited the (something hanging over, or threatening) storm.

dependent (impending) suspend

5. I bought my father some red (devices that hang from the shoulders and hold pants up) for his birthday.

pendulous (suspenders) independents

6. My grandmother is a very (not needing to hang on to others) woman.

dependable suspended (independent)

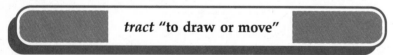
tract "to draw or move"

7. Cats can (draw back) their claws.

detract (retract) subtract

8. Colleen has a stubborn, (unable to be moved) personality, don't you think?

(intractable) distracting tractable

9. Cory was in (a device for pulling on the muscles) after his accident.

retractor tractor (traction)

• • • A FALL FROM THE SKY • • •

Name _____

A. Read each sentence. Underline the word or group of words that explains the boldface word.

1. The **fresco** gleamed in the sun, and I tried to imagine the artist who had created the <u>wall painting</u>.

2. It pictured two mythical figures who, as **fugitives,** dressed themselves in bird feathers to attempt to <u>flee to safety</u>.

3. The painting first shows their <u>rejoicing</u> faces **exulting** in their escape as they soar like birds.

4. Suddenly a **torrential** rain <u>pours down</u>, so <u>heavy</u> that it strips the feathers from their bodies and causes the fugitives to plunge to earth.

5. The picture is **beguiling,** because although the theme is loss and death, <u>the viewer is delighted with the beauty and artistry</u> of the work.

B. Use each of the boldface words in a sentence of your own.
Sentences will vary.

1. _____

_____

2. _____

_____

3. _____

_____

4. _____

_____

5. _____

_____

• • • A FALL FROM THE SKY • • •

Name _____

Complete the cause-and-effect diagram.
   Accept reasonable responses. Possible answers are provided.

WHAT DAEDALUS DOES	WHAT HAPPENS AS A RESULT
kills Talos out of jealousy	is imprisoned and exiled
rebuilds king's palace	enjoys honor and prestige
goes against King Minos	becomes a fugitive
makes wings to escape	masters skill of flight

WHAT ICARUS DOES	WHAT HAPPENS AS A RESULT
decides to help his father	collects feathers
loves flying	forgets his father's warning
ignores his father's warning	flies too close to the sun
the sun melts his wings	falls into the sea and drowns

• • • A FALL FROM THE SKY • • •

Name _____

All the words in the box come from the names of Greek and Roman gods and goddesses. Use the words to complete the passages.

Atlantic	martial	geography	hygiene	janitor
January	volcano	atlas	psychology	cereal

Roman Mythology

1. Janus was the two-headed god who looked both ways and who guarded gates and doors. A person who takes care of buildings and doors is called a _____**janitor**_____. _____**January**_____ is the month that looks forward to one year and back to the previous year.

2. Vulcan, the god of fire, lived deep in the earth. When he was angry, he spewed hot lava up through the earth and formed a _____**volcano**_____.

3. Ceres, the goddess of agriculture, gave her name to a common grain product, _____**cereal**_____.

4. Mars, the fierce god of war, has given his name to warlike military music. We call this type of music _____**martial**_____.

Greek Mythology

5. Atlas, the god of great strength, held the world on his shoulders. A book containing maps of the world is an _____**atlas**_____, while the _____**Atlantic**_____ is one of the great oceans of the world.

6. Gaea was the goddess of earth. The study and description of the earth's surface is called _____**geography**_____.

7. Psyche was the goddess of the mind and soul. Today, the science and study of the mind is called _____**psychology**_____.

8. Hygeia was the goddess of health. We study good health today through the science of _____**hygiene**_____.

• • • A FALL FROM THE SKY • • •

Name _____

Use the map, map legend, compass rose, and distance scale to answer the questions.

1. What small sea is found to the east of Greece? To the west?

the Aegean Sea; the Ionian Sea
_____

2. What large island is part of Greece? In which direction does it lie from the mainland?

Crete; south/southeast
_____

3. About how many kilometers is the Greek mainland from north to south? What is this measurement in miles?

about 500 kilometers; about 300 miles
_____

4. What is the capital of Greece? **Athens**
_____

5. If you wished to sail from Athens to the port of Khania on Crete, how many kilometers would the ship have to travel?

about 280 kilometers
_____

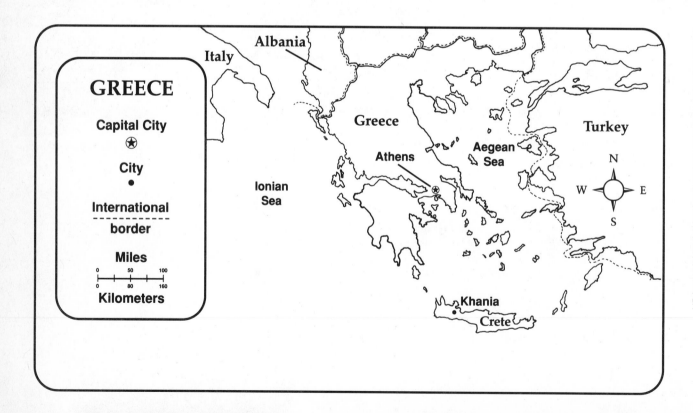

• • • A FALL FROM THE SKY • • •

Name _____

A. Read the following similes and answer the questions about each one.

> **Her laughter was like a bubbling brook.**

1. What two things are being compared?
someone's laughter and a brook

2. Which sense is appealed to in the simile?
sense of hearing—the way the laughter sounds

3. How does the girl's laughter sound?
Students may suggest it sounds merry, light, and so on.

> **In his grief, Jeff's face was as frozen as a stone.**

4. What two things are being compared?
Jeff's face and a stone

5. Which sense is appealed to in the simile?
the sense of sight—the way Jeff's face looks

6. What does Jeff's face look like?
Students may suggest it looks hard, without feeling or motion.

B. Complete the following similes. **Responses will vary.**

1. His voice was as harsh as _____.

2. The cold green lake was like _____.

3. Her well-scrubbed hands smelled like _____.

4. The opposing team was as agile as _____.

5. Biting into the ripe peach was like _____.

• • • THE FORCE OF LUCK • • •

Name _____

A. Complete the story by writing a word from the box on each line.

> respective   contends   squandered
> spendthrift   benefactors   intact

Once a king and a queen had a large fortune. They wished to keep

it ____**intact**____, not to spend it at all, and bequeath it to their

son and their daughter.

   Sadly, each one ____**squandered**____ his or her part of the

fortune until very little was left. Both had spent the money on their

____**respective**____ passions. The queen spent her half on rare

artworks, while the king spent his half on thoroughbred horses. Then

each accused the other of being an irresponsible ____**spendthrift**____.

   "Our accountant ____**contends**____ that if we had invested

the money, we would now be very rich. We could have doubled our

fortune to leave to our children," moaned the queen.

   "Oh, where shall we find kind ____**benefactors**____ to give

us the money we have lost?" whined the king.

B. Write each word in the box on the line next to its meaning.

1. ____**squandered**____ spent wastefully

2. ____**contends**____ argues

3. ____**benefactors**____ givers of help, especially financial

4. ____**intact**____ untouched, whole

5. ____**spendthrift**____ person who wastes money

6. ____**respective**____ particular, individual

••• THE FORCE OF LUCK •••

Name _____

Fill in the sequence diagram. **Accept reasonable responses.**

BEGINNING

FIRST, **the miller gets $200. A hawk steals it.**

NEXT, **the miller gets $200 more. His wife trades it away in a jar of bran.**

THEN, **the miller gets lead; gives lead to fisherman; gets fish; sells diamond; becomes prosperous.**

ENDING

FINALLY, **the lost money turns up.**

Name _____

Read each numbered sentence and notice the underlined word. Then circle the definition that best fits the word as it is used in the sentence.

1. After she and her partner discussed the <u>matter</u>, the store owner decided to expand.

   a. material that makes up everything in the universe
   b. (concern, affair)
   c. to be important

2. <u>Store</u> the valuables in the safe.

   a. place where goods are sold
   b. supply
   c. (to put in a place for safekeeping)

3. We won't be able to <u>settle</u> this argument if you leave.

   a. to sink to the bottom
   b. (to resolve)
   c. to establish homes in a place

4. It seems to be Jamie's <u>lot</u> to have people depend on him.

   a. (fate)
   b. plot of land
   c. one's share or portion

5. Yolanda is always laughing, and I doubt she will ever <u>change</u>.

   a. coins of small amount
   b. (to become different)
   c. to put on different clothing

SUMMARIZING
the **L**EARNING

Some words have _____**multiple**_____ meanings. To determine

which _____**meaning**_____ is intended, look at how the word is

_____**used in the sentence**_____.

• • • THE FORCE OF LUCK • • •

Name _____

Read the folktale and complete the exercise.

There once were two brothers who lived in a far-off land. Homer, the older, was handsome and could easily have been a movie star, except there were no movies in those days. So he had to be content with seeing how the village lasses looked his way with approving eyes. Homer was also as smart as a whip and could easily have been a Ph.D., except there were no advanced degrees in those days. So he had to be content with reading books in Greek and Latin.

His brother, Gomer, was as plain as a post. The lasses who smiled at Homer frowned on Gomer. Gomer was also none too bright, so while Homer was reading his Greek and Latin, Gomer struggled to read the road signs between their home and the town.

One day an old beggar came knocking at the brothers' door. "May I have but a crust of bread and a sip of milk?" he implored.

"You'll be off with neither!" shouted Homer. "Do you think we've nothing better to do than feed lazy beggars? Begone!"

But Gomer intervened. "Here, sir, please take whatever you wish, for you look as though you have had a long journey." And Gomer gave the beggar his own dinner.

At this the beggar stood tall and threw off his rags. "I am King John of this region," he intoned. "And I can see that I have very different people as my subjects. You," he pointed to Homer, "will keep your handsomeness, but the lasses will look on you and be ill. And you, kind one," he said to Gomer, "will remain plain, yet win the love of all who know you." And so it came to pass.

1. List three characteristics of Homer.
handsome, smart, cruel, or selfish

2. List three characteristics of Gomer.
plain, dull-witted, kind, or generous

3. Make a judgment based upon your description of the two brothers.
Accept reasonable responses: Looks and brains are not as important as

character. There are different ways of being "handsome."

Name _____

Read the sentences. Underline the correct meaning for the boldface word in each sentence.

1. "I'm sick of these **archaic** customs," stormed Rayla. "It's time for some new ideas!"

    novel   famous   <u>ancient</u>   original

2. It was Rayla's **fervid** hope that a woman would be allowed to rule her father's kingdom, and that she would be the first.

    forlorn   disgruntled   questionable   <u>eager</u>

3. A **precedent** for male rule had been set thousands of years before, and until now no one had sought to break it.

    <u>model</u>   king   judge   request

4. Rayla had challenged this rule as **discreetly** as she could up until now, but it was time to be more aggressive and to say something openly.

    angrily   <u>carefully</u>   radically   hopefully

5. She didn't want to bring **havoc** on the kingdom with her demands, but she wished for some things to change.

    questions   laughter   <u>great confusion</u>   shame

6. She had heard **grisly** stories of people in earlier times who had dared to bring about change, and they had been swiftly exiled or killed.

    <u>gruesome</u>   happy   exciting   puzzling

7. As she thought over her problem, Rayla and her hunting dog **scrabbled** up a deserted rocky hillside looking for dragons.

    <u>scraped or pawed</u>   leapt joyfully   flew   climbed quickly

8. "Perhaps if I could **vanquish** a giant dragon all by myself, they would listen to me," Rayla thought.

    release   find   tame   <u>defeat</u>

9. She bent and stretched her **supple** body and pulled out her sword so that she would be ready to attack.

    <u>flexible</u>   armored   tired   ancient

Name _____

Complete the preview-prediction chart. **Accept reasonable responses.**
Possible answers are provided.

What I know from the beginning . . .
**Aerin is a fifteen-year-old girl who is the highest ranking female
in the kingdom, but she cannot inherit the throne because she is
a girl. Her cousin Tor is the heir to the throne.**

What I learn later . . .
**Aerin reads old books about dragons. She also finds an old
formula for a fireproof ointment that she succeeds in making.
When a small dragon harasses a village, Aerin rides out alone
on her father's war-horse to slay the dragon.**

I predict that . . .
**Aerin will succeed in slaying the dragon and will become a hero
to her father and inherit the kingdom.**

What really happened . . .
**Aerin sets out for the village alone before the hunters. She
succeeds in battling two dragons and amazes the village people
and her father's hunters.**

• • • THE HERO AND THE CROWN • • •

Name _____

Read the passage and complete the exercise.

Far off over the sea there were two villages that were plagued by monsters. The village of Freeland sat at the top of a mountain. Its people made their living by farming and herding goats on the mountainside. An old monster named Gog lived in a cave in the mountain. Every month or so he would fly from his cave, steal a couple of plump, valuable goats for food, and disappear into his lair. To stop Gog, the Freelanders offered him different foods—tomatoes, rutabagas, and fresh fruit. But he was uninterested. Finally, they offered him one of their large delicious pumpkins. His eyes lit up as he tasted it. "Bring me one hundred of these every month and your goats are safe," he growled. The people of Freeland happily agreed.

At the bottom of the mountain nestled the village of Treeland. Its inhabitants were farmers who also fished in the Crystal River. The monster who plagued Treeland swam in the river. Mog, as he was called, came out of the river periodically to carry off crops of corn and beans. The people of Treeland were angered by this and decided to poison the monster. They filled the river with every noxious chemical they could find. Well, Mog perished all right, but so did the village, because all the fish died as well as the crops, which were irrigated by the poisoned water from the river.

1. Compare and contrast the two villages.

Freeland—at top of mountain, people farm and herd. Treeland—at bottom of

mountain, people farm and fish.

2. Compare and contrast the two monsters.

Gog of Freeland lives in a cave, can fly, eats goats. Mog of Treeland lives in a

river, can swim, eats crops.

3. Compare and contrast the ways the villages solve their problem.

Freeland finds something else for Gog to eat. Treeland poisons Mog and

accidentally kills everything else as well.

4. Make a judgment based on your information.

Accept reasonable responses: Destroying your enemy can result in

destroying yourself.

• • • THE HERO AND THE CROWN • • •

Name _____

A. Read each example of figurative language. Tell what two things are being compared in each example.

1. As I walked through the deserted alley, I could feel the fear coiled in my stomach, waiting to strike.

fear and a snake _____

2. When Jean got news of her prize, her heart swelled inside her, ready to burst.

a heart and a balloon being blown up _____

3. The old cars sat on their haunches, guarding the junkyard.

cars and guard dogs _____

4. The withered tree moaned in the wind and waved its feeble arms against the sky.

a tree and a sick person _____

5. Jed slept poorly because of the stabbing pain from his broken leg.

pain and a knife _____

B. Write an example of figurative language to describe each of the following. **Examples will vary.**

1. a violent storm _____

2. a fretful baby _____

3. a broken piece of machinery _____

4. a disappointed person _____

5. a sunset or a sunrise _____

••• THE HERO AND THE CROWN •••

Name _____

Complete each sentence by using a prefix or a suffix and the underlined root word in the parentheses to create a new word. Write the new word in the blank. Choose from the prefixes *il-, im-, in-, ir-, un-, dis-,* and the suffix *-less,* all of which mean "not" or "without."

1. The small bird remained (not <u>mobile</u>) to fool the searching hawk.
   immobile

2. Do you (not <u>approve</u>) of my science project? **disapprove**

3. Every time a factory closes, there are more (without a <u>job</u>) people.
   jobless

4. The candidate ran (not <u>opposed</u>) for the mayor's seat.
   unopposed

5. Crossing against the light is (not <u>legal</u>). **illegal**

6. Your information is interesting but (not <u>relevant</u>) to the topic.
   irrelevant

7. Hallie dislikes doing (not <u>perfect</u>) work of any kind.
   imperfect

8. Samson has been (not <u>contented</u>) ever since he moved to a new town.
   discontented

9. We worried about Wally's behavior because it was so (not <u>consistent</u>).
   inconsistent

10. Even though Margo is smart, she often feels (not <u>competent</u>).
    incompetent

11. Until her health improved, Carla felt (without <u>hope</u>).
    hopeless

12. It is unlike Jake to be so (not <u>responsible</u>). **irresponsible**

• • • THE HERO AND THE CROWN • • •

Name _____

Read this sample page from the index of an imaginary book on dragons.
Then answer the questions.

D

Dragon births, 40, 42–45

Dragon keeping, 45–50

Dragons

    deaths of fictional, 113, 125–130, 355

    history of, 1–20, 31–34

    names of in literature

        Firebreather, 55

        Fire Wind, 60

        Sweetfire, 51

Dragon's Blood, 210. *See also author* Yolen, Jane.

Dragon training, 100–118

1. You are interested in finding out the history of dragons. Under what

    entry would you find this information? **under the entry *Dragons, history of***

    On what pages is this information? **pages 1–20 and 31–34**

2. You remember a dragon named Sweetfire from a story you read but
cannot remember the book's title. On what page might you find a

    reference to the book? **page 51**

3. What is the first page that contains information on the births of

    dragons? **page 40**

4. On what page would you look to find out about the book *Dragon's*

    Blood? **page 210**

5. Where in the index would you look for information on the author of

    Dragon's Blood? **under Y, for the author *Yolen, Jane***

Name _____

Read the following paragraphs. Circle the context clues that helped you determine the meaning of each underlined word. Then write each word on the line next to its meaning.

Thunder (rumbled) ominously and lightning (flashed) in the (darkening) distance. Mara pulled her jacket more tightly around her. The bad weather had been relentless; (almost every day) had been stormy with heavy rain and high winds. (Rain) had often deluged the island, (flooding) the path Mara took to walk home from school.

Each high storm tide left a residue of dark (sand, driftwood, and shells) along the shore. Everybody on the island recounted their (stories of flooding over and over again.)

Mara paused by the beach on the lee side of a small hill to see whether any pretty shells had lodged in the (calm, sheltered) water. Something (moved) (just at the edge) of her peripheral vision, and she (swung around to stare directly) at an approaching waterspout. The terrifying funnel of whirling water roared toward her.

Just in time, the waterspout turned back seaward, but the (heavy rain) cascaded (down) on Mara. "That was close," she gasped, and the loud expulsion of air told her she had been (holding her breath) for a long time.

1. told _____**recounted**_____

2. flowed heavily _____**cascaded**_____

3. remainder _____**residue**_____

4. near the outer edges _____**peripheral**_____

5. a forcing out _____**expulsion**_____

6. in a threatening manner _____**ominously**_____

7. flooded _____**deluged**_____

8. unforgiving _____**relentless**_____

9. sheltered _____**lee**_____

THE TALKING EARTH

Name _____

Fill in the narrative elements chart.

SETTING

Time: present—before, during, and after a hurricane

Place: Florida Everglades

CHARACTERS

Billie Wind: a 13-year-old Seminole girl stranded in the Florida Everglades	**Oats Tiger:** a 12-year-old Seminole boy on a quest for a new name
Burden: Billie Wind's turtle	**Coootchobee:** a panther Billie Wind kept as a kitten

PLOT

Conflict: Billie Wind must figure out how to survive the storm.

Resolution: Coootchobee and Burden help Billie and Oats survive the storm and teach them about loving the earth.

Name _____

Read each dictionary entry. Note how the same word is used in different ways. Then read the sentences below each entry. Use the sentence context to determine the way the word is used. Write the number of the correct definition in the space.

meet [mēt] **1** *v.* to come face to face with. **2** *v.* to keep an appointment with. **3** *n.* a meeting, as for a sports event. **4** *v.* to be introduced or become acquainted.

4 1. I would like you to *meet* Jane.

3 2. Mandrell is competing in next week's track *meet*.

1 3. He happened to *meet* his friend at the mall.

2 4. I'll *meet* you at the restaurant.

mind [mīnd] **1** *n.* the part of a person that thinks, feels, remembers, and imagines. **2** *n.* sanity or reason. **3** *v.* to obey. **4** *v.* to object to.

2 5. The pounding music was so loud I thought I would lose my *mind*.

4 6. Do you *mind* if I open the window?

1 7. My grandfather is over eighty, but his *mind* is as clear and sharp as mine is.

3 8. My brother rarely *minds* me when I tell him to do something.

bay [bā] **1** *n.* a body of water partly enclosed by land. **2** *n.* a deep cry, as of hunting dogs. **3** *n.* an evergreen tree with shiny, sweet-smelling leaves. **4** *n.* a reddish-brown horse.

4 9. The *bay* raced across the pasture and neighed.

1 10. The tide comes into the *bay* so fast that swimmers have to be careful.

2 11. He heard the *bay* of the kennel hounds a block away.

3 12. Grandma likes to sit under her *bay* tree.

Name _____

A. Use the Dewey Decimal System to determine where you would find books on each topic listed below. Write the numbers and the name of the category on the line.

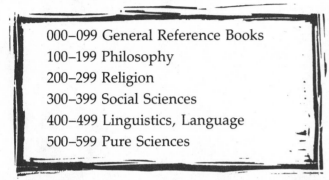

> 000–099 General Reference Books
> 100–199 Philosophy
> 200–299 Religion
> 300–399 Social Sciences
> 400–499 Linguistics, Language
> 500–599 Pure Sciences

> 600–699 Applied Sciences
> 700–799 Arts, Recreation
> 800–899 Literature
> 900–999 History, Geography, Travel

1. Books about crocodiles and alligators **500–599 Pure Sciences**

2. Books about filmmaking **700–799 Arts, Recreation**

3. Collections of plays **800–899 Literature**

4. Books about Australia **900–999 History, Geography, Travel**

5. Books about word origins **400–499 Linguistics, Language**

B. Write on the line the letter and the name of the correct Library of Congress classification for each book title below.

A General Works	G Geography, Anthropology	M Music
B Philosophy, Religion	H Social Sciences	N Fine Arts
C History	J Political Science	P Language, Literature
D Foreign History	K Law	Q Science
E, F American History	L Education	R Medicine

1. *The First Heart Transplant* **R, Medicine**

2. *Schooling in Japan* **L, Education**

3. *Amazon—the Mighty River* **G, Geography, Anthropology**

4. *Greece During the Golden Age* **D, Foreign History**

5. *Neptune—the Blue Planet* **Q, Science**

Name _____

A. Read each sentence. Underline the word or group of words that explains the boldface word.

1. Many scientific theories that were once thought to be **preposterous** are not considered absurd or worthy of scorn any longer.

2. A workable theory is much like a puzzle whose pieces must be **painstakingly** fitted together until the carefully done work pays off.

3. **Remnants** from one civilization may be found near the fragments of another, showing that they were at one time connected in some way.

4. Dam-like structures in the **vicinity** of dry, parched land tell us that the region nearby was once a lake or perhaps completely covered with water.

5. Early civilizations have been **engulfed** by lava flows, floods, or other disasters, and their secrets remain swallowed up forever.

6. On occasion, however, we can excavate the remains of a city ruined by one of these **devastating** events and learn how the people attempted to cope with the destructive forces of nature.

B. Write six sentences of your own using each of the boldface words. **Sentences will vary.**

1. _____

2. _____

3. _____

4. _____

5. _____

6. _____

Name _____

Fill in the SQ3R chart. **Accept reasonable responses.**

SURVEY **This selection talks about the crust of the earth. Its giant plates move, causing earthquakes and volcanoes.**

QUESTION	PREDICTED ANSWER	READ
What are superislands?		

RECITE	REVIEW

Name _____

Read the directions for patching a hole in a bicycle tire. Then answer the questions.

The process of patching a bicycle tire can be divided into four parts. First, remove the wheel from the bicycle. Then remove the tire from the rim. This allows you to take the tube from inside the tire.

Second, find the leak. Gently squeeze all around the tube until you hear the hiss of escaping air. This action pinpoints the puncture, or hole.

Third, repair the leak. Sand the area around the hole, and make the area as free of dirt particles as you can. Then apply rubber glue around the hole, and allow it to dry for a minute. Finally, apply a patch to the area, and let it dry until it is stuck tight.

Fourth, replace the tube inside the tire, and reattach the tire to the wheel. Put the wheel back on the bike.

Well, there is a fifth step, but it's pretty obvious. What do you think it is?

1. How many basic parts are described in the process? __4_____

2. Which part involves squeezing the tube? __the second part, finding the leak___

3. Which part involves sanding the area around the hole? __the third part, patching the__ __leak_____

4. Why do you think the area around the hole has to be cleaned off after sanding? __The glue and patch will stick better if the area is clean.___

5. What is done in the fifth step? __Fill the tire with air._____

6. Choose one of the four parts and restate it in your own words. __Wording will vary.___

SUMMARIZING *the* **L**EARNING

When giving directions, divide the task into __several__ steps.
To show the __order__ of steps, use __time__ words.
Explain unfamiliar __words or terms__.

Name _____

An eighth-grade class conducted a survey to see what kinds of jobs its students took to earn money. The results are found in the bar graph. Use the graph to answer the questions.

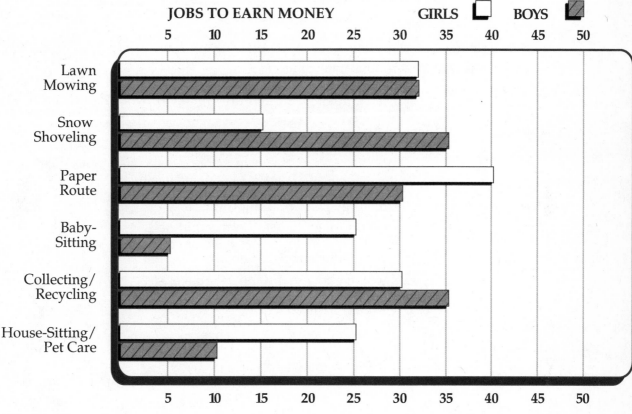

JOBS TO EARN MONEY   GIRLS ☐   BOYS ▨

1. Approximately how many girls earn money mowing lawns? _____**30**_____

   Boys? _____**30**_____

2. How many girls have a paper route? _____**40**_____ Boys? _____**30**_____

3. In which three jobs do girls outnumber boys? _**paper route, baby-sitting, and**_ **house-sitting/pet care**

4. In which two jobs do boys outnumber girls? _**snow shoveling and**_ **collecting/recycling**

5. What is the total number of eighth-grade boys and girls who collect materials for recycling? _____**65**_____

Name _____

A. Complete the story by writing a word from the box on each line.

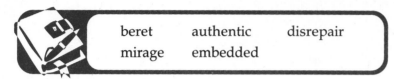

| beret | authentic | disrepair |
| mirage | embedded | |

After the earthquake and the seismic wave that followed, most of the homes on the island were in a state of total
_____**disrepair**_____. Several small boats had been driven inland by the huge wave and were now _____**embedded**_____ in the high sandy hills.

The photographer pulled his _____**beret**_____ tighter over his head and snapped picture after picture. The devastation was so complete that when he came upon an intact house, he thought he was looking at a _____**mirage**_____. The images of destruction that he captured in his photographs would show that the earthquake was an _____**authentic**_____ catastrophe.

B. Write each word from the box on the line next to its meaning.

1. _____**beret**_____ soft, flat, round cap

2. _____**disrepair**_____ bad condition

3. _____**embedded**_____ fixed firmly in something

4. _____**mirage**_____ illusion

5. _____**authentic**_____ genuine

• • • WHAT THE TWISTER DID • • •

Name _____

Fill in the humor-prediction chart. **Accept reasonable responses.**
Examples are provided.

	WHAT THE TWISTER DID	WHY IT WAS FUNNY
Predicted Event	moved things all over town	exaggeration no one was hurt
Actual Event	blew trophy man into bottle	an odd coincidence
Predicted Event		
Actual Event		
Predicted Event		
Actual Event		
Predicted Event		
Actual Event		

• • • WHAT THE TWISTER DID • • •

Name _____

A. Read each of the advertisements. Decide which *two* of the following techniques each advertisement uses and write your answer on the line.

Ad techniques

slanted language (glad words/sad words), testimonial, snob appeal, bandwagon

1. Are you the *only one* on your block who hasn't tried Glow-Bright Toothpaste? No *wonder* you sit *alone* while everyone else has fun. Stop being a *loser* and join the *happy* crowd, the *alive* crowd, the *in* crowd! Smile your way to popularity with Glow-Bright!
glad words, sad words; bandwagon

2. JoAnn Veryrich appears *exclusively* in George Arbany clothing. What better reason can you *need* for wearing these *smart outfits* that will make you stand out from the *ordinary* folk! Says JoAnn, "Arbany clothing makes me feel as if I'm wearing *money,* it's so fabulous!"
testimonial; snob appeal

3. Want to feel like the *greatest*? Wish for people to *flock* to you? It's easy, with Old Salt After-Shave Lotion. You'll be everyone's *dream man.* Other men won't have a *chance* after you walk into a room. *Only* the *finest* wear Old Salt, so be sure you *qualify*!
glad words, sad words; snob appeal

B. Write a short advertisement of your own, using at least *two* of the techniques on this page to describe your product.
Accept reasonable responses.

_____

_____

_____

_____

Name _____

Read each numbered sentence and notice the underlined word. Then choose the definition that best fits the word as it is used in the sentence. Circle the letter next to that definition.

1. The heavy plastic <u>shade</u> came crashing down during a violent wind.

   a. area of darkness, as under a tree
   (b.) device for a window or door, to cut off light
   c. small difference in color, as shades of green

2. The driver signaled before he made a <u>right</u> turn.

   a. correct or accurate
   b. something claimed, as a right to free speech
   (c.) toward the right, the opposite of left

3. The loud <u>beat</u> from the stereo next door kept me from sleeping.

   (a.) rhythm
   b. to defeat, as in a sports event
   c. to stir or mix, as in baking

4. We rented a <u>crane</u> to lift the steel beams.

   a. long-necked wading bird
   (b.) machine for moving heavy objects
   c. to stretch one's neck, to try to see

5. We would have been cut off even from radio news during the flood except for our local <u>hams</u>.

   (a.) amateur radio operators
   b. meat cuts of a hog
   c. actors who overdo their roles

6. During the movie, we all had to <u>draw</u> a breath when the car sailed over the cliff.

   a. to pull down, out, together, or back
   (b.) to inhale
   c. to make (a picture or a sketch)

WHAT THE TWISTER DID

Name _____

Read the article on these two pages, and fill in the missing entries in
the outlines.

HURRICANES

I. Names of Storm

   A. **Americas—taken from Taino Indian word *hurakán***

   B. North Pacific—typhoon

   C. **Indian Ocean and South Pacific-cyclone**

II. What They Do (Characteristics)

   A. Form over tropical areas

      1. eye

      2. **wall clouds**

   B. Swirling winds move over wide area

      1. **counterclockwise in Northern Hemisphere**

      2. **clockwise in Southern Hemisphere**

   C. Speed/Effects

      1. Wall clouds reach 130–150 miles per hour

      2. **Whole storm moves at 20–30 miles per hour**

      3. Causes coastal and island destruction

The hurricane is one of the most violent and destructive storms on earth. The name of this storm in the Americas comes from a Taino Indian word, *hurakán*. In the North Pacific the same type of storm is called a *typhoon*. In the Indian and South Pacific oceans it is called a *cyclone*.

No matter what its name, the hurricane forms and travels in the same way. Areas of low pressure form over oceans in the tropics. In the Northern Hemisphere the winds begin to swirl counterclockwise around a center of calm, called the *eye* (clockwise in the Southern Hemisphere). At the height of the storm, the winds of the *wall clouds*, which surround the eye, can reach 130–150 miles per hour or higher. As the storm moves, at about 20–30 miles per hour, it gets larger and much stronger, causing widespread destruction in coastal and island areas.

Name _____

As a hurricane moves over the sea, its winds create heavy *storm surges,* ocean waves which are far above normal height. Storm surges flood land areas and, combined with a high tide, can be particularly devastating. Hurricanes eventually hit land, where they cause heavy rain and windstorms. Then they blow themselves out and move out to sea, greatly weakened.

The hurricane season in the North Atlantic generally lasts from June to November. Each season the storms are named with either women's or men's names in alphabetical order as they occur. Some hurricanes, such as *Camille* and *Hugo,* were so destructive that their names will never be forgotten by the people who lived through them.

People often compare hurricanes with tornadoes because both cause so much damage. Some say tornadoes are more destructive. Tornadoes can be more intense and do stranger things, it is true. They are unpredictable, while hurricanes can be tracked and people can be warned. But in the final analysis they must be considered less destructive simply because they are so much smaller than hurricanes in area. Their fearsomeness comes from the fact that they can hit—hopscotch style—in several different places very quickly, taking people by surprise.

D. Progress
1. Creates storm surges at sea
2. **Causes wind and rainstorms on land**
3. **Blows self out over land, moves back to sea**

III. Additional Facts
A. **Hurricane season in Atlantic from June to November**
B. **Named for women or men**
C. Some names remembered for their destructiveness

IV. **Comparisons with Tornadoes**
A. Hurricane
1. moves over wider area
2. **is predictable**
B. **Tornado**
1. **moves over small area**
2. is unpredictable

• • • MEN FROM EARTH • • •

Name _____

Read the sentences. Underline the correct meaning for the boldface word
in each sentence.

1. The crew members sighed with relief as they realized they would soon
terminate their long space journey.

    <u>end</u>   begin   regret   replay

2. They had flown past many **exotic**-looking planets, as different from
earth as one could imagine.

    small   familiar   <u>strange</u>   threatening

3. They were ready to **deploy** their weapons if they saw signs of danger
on the planet they were approaching.

    destroy quickly   repair   discard   <u>put into position</u>

4. The pilot plotted a **trajectory** that would take the ship in a sweeping
arc down to the surface of the planet.

    grid   rocket   story   <u>curving path</u>

5. The crew members took their landing positions just as they had
pretended to do during their **simulation** back on earth.

    <u>practice run</u>   takeoff   slow orbit   nap

6. As they neared the planet, they could see the dry, **corrugated** surface,
which might cause a landing problem.

    smooth   <u>ridged</u>   watery   red

7. Their excitement caused a surge of adrenalin, which altered their
physiology from a state of rest to a state of energy.

    space suits   dreams   minds   <u>functions of organisms</u>

8. As the ship landed, the crew members felt several **spasms** run
through it before it settled onto the surface.

    <u>shudders</u>   breakdowns   photographs   radio blackouts

9. The crew members had each brought **mementos** to leave on the planet
as a sign of their visit.

    clothing   hiking boots   tents   <u>reminders</u>

10. The pilot had brought some **shrapnel** that had been removed from his
leg in a hospital in Vietnam.

    shoes   thorns   crutches   <u>bombshell fragments</u>

• • • MEN FROM EARTH • • •

Name _____

Fill in the SQ3R chart. **Accept reasonable responses.**

SURVEY "Men from Earth" is an account of the mission of Apollo 11, the first manned spacecraft to land on the moon.

QUESTION	PREDICTED ANSWER	READ
What happened to the astronauts at Kennedy Space Center on July 16, 1969?		

RECITE	REVIEW

Name _____

Read the sentences. Then decide which of the written-out phrases in the box represents the acronym or abbreviation in each sentence. Write the correct phrase on the line.

Congress of Racial Equality

National Aeronautics and Space Administration

North Atlantic Treaty Organization

Scholastic Aptitude Test

Self-Contained Underwater Breathing Apparatus

United Nations International Children's Emergency Fund

World Health Organization

Zone Improvement Plan

1. Kal is studying madly for his SAT this weekend.
Scholastic Aptitude Test
_____

2. Rini is saving money to buy herself scuba-diving equipment.
Self-Contained Underwater Breathing Apparatus
_____

3. Vanessa worked for CORE during the equal-rights demonstrations.
Congress of Racial Equality
_____

4. Remember to add the ZIP code when addressing an envelope.
Zone Improvement Plan
_____

5. The engineers at NASA repaired a shuttle defect.
National Aeronautics and Space Administration
_____

6. We always buy Christmas cards from UNICEF.
United Nations International Children's Emergency Fund
_____

7. The United States, Great Britain, and France were three original members of NATO.
North Atlantic Treaty Organization
_____

8. My aunt is a doctor, and she works for WHO.
World Health Organization
_____

• • • MEN FROM EARTH • • •

Name _____

The first manned spacecraft was *Mercury.* A diagram of the spacecraft is shown. Use it to answer the questions.

1. How long is the spacecraft? __**7 feet**_____

2. Which part protects the spacecraft from the extreme temperature of outer space? Where is it? __**the heat shield; at the back of the spacecraft**__

3. Which part protects the astronaut's atmosphere inside? __**the environmental control**__
   system_____

4. Which part allows the astronaut to leave and enter the spacecraft?
   Where is it? __**the hatch; to the front and right of the astronaut**__

5. Which two parts allow the astronaut to see phenomena outside the
   spacecraft? __**the periscope and the window**__

6. What allows the astronaut to communicate with Earth? __**the communication system**__

7. The nose cone and the antenna housing were designed to fall off
   during the return to Earth. Where are they located? __**at the top of the spacecraft,**__
   above the parachutes_____

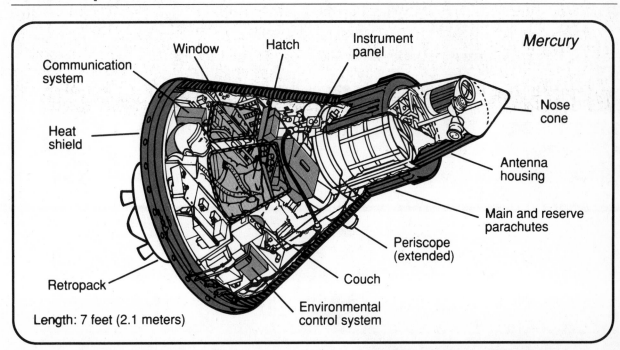

Length: 7 feet (2.1 meters)

• • • Men from Earth • • •

Name _____

Read the passage, and complete the exercises. Circle the letter next to the correct answer. Then tell briefly why the other three choices are wrong.

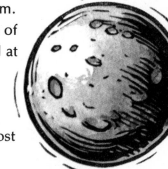

The spacecraft *Voyager* visited the planets Jupiter, Saturn, Uranus, and Neptune and their surroundings from 1977 to 1989. In 1989 *Magellan* was launched. It has brought us news of our cousin planet Venus. Earlier spacecraft explored the surface of Mars.

Until the *Voyager* trek, only Earth was known to have active volcanoes. *Voyager* showed scientists that both Jupiter's hot moon Io and Neptune's freezing satellite Triton have evidence of volcanism. As *Magellan* began to map Venus in 1990, it also found evidence of volcanic activity on that planet. Scientists continue to be amazed at the wealth of information sent to Earth by these nonhuman explorers.

1. On which of the following has volcanic activity been discovered most recently?

A. Mars   (B.) Venus   C. Io   D. Triton

No volcanic activity has been discovered on Mars. Both Io and Triton were

explored by *Voyager*, which finished its explorations in 1989.

2. Which of the following was explored by the *Voyager* spacecraft?

A. Magellan   B. Mars   (C.) Saturn   D. Venus

The *Voyager* spacecraft explored Jupiter, Saturn, Neptune, and Uranus.

***Magellan* is a spacecraft that is exploring Venus.**

3. When did *Magellan* explore Venus?

A. 1977   B. 1980   C. 1989   (D.) 1990

***Magellan* was not launched until 1989. The *Voyager* spacecraft visited**

various planets from 1977 to 1989.

• • • MEN FROM EARTH • • •

Name _____

Use the Greek and Latin roots, the prefixes, and the combining forms in the box to help you complete each exercise. Choose your answer from the words in parentheses. Write your answer on the line.

Greek Roots		Prefixes	
cosmos-	"world"	*de-*	"take away from"
gyros-	"circle"	*re-*	"again"
hydr-	"having to do with water"	*cis-*	"on this side of"
nautes-	"sailor"	*trans-*	"across, through, beyond"
Latin Roots		**Combining Forms**	
altus-	"high"	*-genic*	"suitable for"
luna-	"moon"	*-meter*	"device for measuring"
		-scope	"device for viewing"

1. Americans call an outer-space traveler an astronaut, which means "star sailor." The Soviets call their space traveler a "world sailor," or

   cosmonaut
   _____. (argonaut, cosmonaut)

2. The food in a spacecraft is _____**dehydrated**_____; that is, all the water has been taken out of it. (dehydrated, hydrogen)

3. When the astronauts are ready to eat, they ____**rehydrate**____ the dried food, or add water to it again. (rehydrate, hydrogenate)

4. A ____**gyroscope**____ is a spinning instrument that helps keep airplanes and spacecraft steady. (hydrometer, gyroscope)

5. The deep space void between the earth and the moon is called

   cislunar
   _____ space. (translunar, cislunar)

6. When astronauts wish to know how high they are above a landing spot,

   they use an ____**altimeter**____. (altimeter, lunameter)

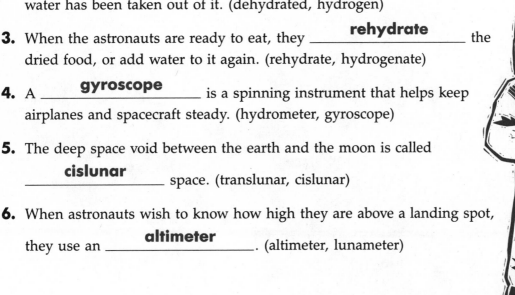

Name _____

Read the following sentences. Use context clues to determine the meaning of each underlined word. Then write each word on the line next to its meaning.

1. The explosion in the factory had left several workers with a complete loss of hearing. Such profound injuries had never happened before.

2. After the injured workers had otherwise recovered, the supervisor of the factory was in turmoil trying to figure out what to do with them. He was afraid he would have to lay them off.

3. Finally, one of the uninjured workers said to him, "You should not have a qualm about keeping our coworkers in their jobs. Their work is sight-oriented, not hearing-oriented."

4. Now a whole line of clothing is made exclusively by the group of hearing-impaired workers, who are proud of their unique accomplishments.

5. "Perhaps we are entering a new epoch of business management," said the supervisor. "This new era would be brighter for every good worker with or without all five senses."

6. _____**qualm**_____ fear or hesitation

7. _____**turmoil**_____ condition of confusion or agitation

8. _____**epoch**_____ period of time, an age

9. _____**exclusively**_____ completely, only

10. _____**profound**_____ deep, complete

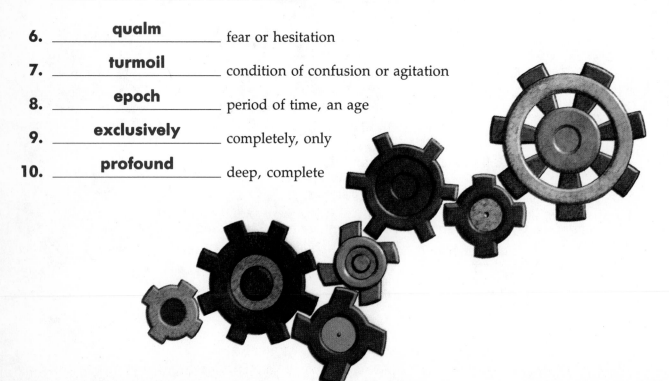

• • • LISTEN FOR THE SINGING • • •

Name _____

Fill in the problem-solution chart. **Accept reasonable responses. Examples are provided.**

CHARACTERS **Anna, Rudi, Mrs. Schumacher**	SETTING **Toronto, Canada; autumn 1940**
Predicted Problem **Rudi is blind.**	Actual Problem **Rudi is in despair about his blindness and will not talk about it or accept help.**
Predicted Solution **Anna will help him.**	Actual Solution **Anna forces Rudi to accept help by shocking him into facing his situation.**
Predicted Problem	Actual Problem
Predicted Solution	Actual Solution

• • • LISTEN FOR THE SINGING • • •

Name _____

Look at the synonyms for each boldface word. Decide which of the three synonyms carries the mildest connotation (1), which carries the strongest connotation (10), and which falls in the middle (5). Write each of the words in the correct blank below the scale.

1. poor: awful, imperfect, worthless

1 <========================== 5 ==========================> 10
    imperfect   **awful**   **worthless**

2. confusion: chaos, puzzlement, uproar

1 <========================== 5 ==========================> 10
    puzzlement   **uproar**   **chaos**

3. good: fine, superb, satisfactory

1 <========================== 5 ==========================> 10
    satisfactory   **fine**   **superb**

4. surprise: astound, startle, astonish

1 <========================== 5 ==========================> 10
    startle   **astonish**   **astound**

5. nervous: restless, overwrought, tense

1 <========================== 5 ==========================> 10
    restless   **tense**   **overwrought**

6. cry: shriek, sob, whimper

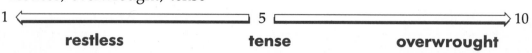

1 <========================== 5 ==========================> 10
    whimper   **sob**   **shriek**

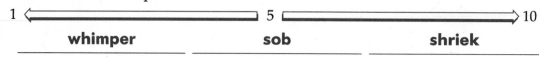

• • • LISTEN FOR THE SINGING • • •

Name _____

Read the words and their several meanings below. Then decide which meaning of the word is used in the sentence. Write the correct number in the blank.

> **grade: 1.** any one division of elementary or high school; **2.** slope of a road or railroad track; **3.** a degree in rank or quality.

_____1_____ 1. When Anna was in ninth *grade*, Rudi enlisted in the navy.

> **shed: 1.** a building used for storage; **2.** to get rid of; **3.** to pour out.

_____3_____ 2. She looked shocked but she *shed* no tears.

> **fault: 1.** flaw, defect; **2.** cause for blame; **3.** a break in the earth's crust.

_____2_____ 3. It was no one's *fault*; it was an accident.

> **deal: 1.** to take positive action; **2.** to carry on business; **3.** to distribute playing cards.

_____1_____ 4. I have to learn to *deal* with my temper.

> **mean: 1.** halfway between two extremes; **2.** signify; **3.** cruel.

_____3_____ 5. Rudi was *mean* to Anna when she was young.

> **relief: 1.** change of persons on duty or watch; **2.** food or money given to needy persons; **3.** lessening of pain or distress.

_____3_____ 6. Anna felt *relief* when Rudi agreed to learn Braille.

Name _____

Read the paragraphs, and answer the questions.

Angelo and Ben are both fourteen-year-old students at the Carlisle School for Oral Language. Both boys are hearing-impaired. Angelo was born deaf, while Ben lost his hearing at age twelve as a result of a severe infection. Both boys know sign language and are learning to communicate orally.

Angelo has been in school for several years and is just beginning to be able to pronounce basic words. Ben, who remembers how words sound and how it feels to speak, is progressing much faster.

When the boys finish practicing their mouth and throat exercises, they chatter away at high speed in sign language.

1. Compare and contrast Ben and Angelo.

Students' answers may vary slightly. Angelo is fourteen years old, deaf since

birth, studies at Carlisle, uses sign well, just beginning to use basic oral

language. Ben is fourteen, lost hearing from infection at twelve, studies at

Carlisle, uses sign well, progressing very rapidly in oral language.

2. Make a judgment based upon the facts about the differences between the boys.

Accept reasonable responses: Someone who loses his hearing later in life

progresses faster when learning oral communication because of recollection

of sounds.

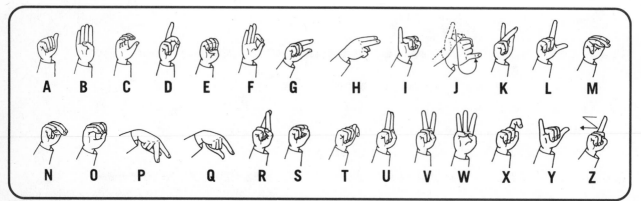

Alphabet courtesy of Gallaudet Press, Washington , D.C. Used with permission.

• • • LISTEN FOR THE SINGING • • •

Name _____

Read the two-sentence items and answer the questions.

> Anna went to the school sports events despite her poor eyesight. Nothing was more exciting than the color and noise of a football game.

1. What is the author's purpose? __to persuade readers that a sports event can be__ __exciting to anyone__

2. What is the author's viewpoint about Anna? __Anna does not let her disability keep__ __her from participating in school events.__

> What happened to Rudi was the worst thing that could happen to any young man. Anna cried for him late at night.

3. What is the author's purpose? __to inform readers that sudden blindness can be__ __devastating__

4. What is the author's viewpoint about Anna? __Anna is compassionate and feels for__ __other people.__

> Rudi reached out to turn on the talking-book machine. This was the best thing that could have happened.

5. What is the author's purpose? __to persuade readers that Rudi's decision was a__ __turning point for him__

6. What is the author's viewpoint about Rudi? __In helping himself, Rudi is beginning__ __to recover his self-respect.__

• • • LITTLE BY LITTLE • • •

Name _____

A. Complete the story by writing a word from the box on each line.

stupefaction	mercenary	grimaced	dubious
lustrous	debonair	affronted	intimidated

Hector had always wanted to be a writer, even though it was an

occupation of _____**dubious**_____ monetary reward. But he soon decided

not to be _____**intimidated**_____ by such concerns. First he wrote about

heroic quests, with men in armor and beautiful women with long

_____**lustrous**_____ hair. No sale. Next he wrote of stylish and

_____**debonair**_____ characters who all spoke in formal language. Still no

takers. Hector was actually _____**affronted**_____ by one publisher's letter

that told him he would never be a writer.

Hector's thoughts soon became more _____**mercenary**_____ as he

realized he needed to make some money soon. He _____**grimaced**_____ as

he saw another publisher's letter in the mail one day, fearing yet another

rejection. So it was with great _____**stupefaction**_____ that Hector read that

his latest work, about camping and backpacking, had been accepted, and he

would be paid shortly.

B. Write the word from the box on the line next to its definition.

1. _____**lustrous**_____ shining

2. _____**stupefaction**_____ astonishment

3. _____**affronted**_____ insulted

4. _____**dubious**_____ doubtful

5. _____**intimidated**_____ frightened or put off

6. _____**debonair**_____ worldly; gracious

7. _____**grimaced**_____ made a face to show disapproval

8. _____**mercenary**_____ greedy

• • • LITTLE BY LITTLE • • •

Name _____

Complete the K-W-L chart. **Responses will vary.**

K	W	L
What I Know	*What I Want to Know*	*What I Learned*
Writers have to sell their work to publishers to make a living.		

• • • LITTLE BY LITTLE • • •

Name _____

Fill in the form for a group you belong to or might like to join. Then answer the questions.

Request Form for Meeting Room

Fill in the form, which is in duplicate, with ball-point pen only. Press hard. Print all information except your signature. **Responses will vary.**

**Name of group requesting
meeting room**   _____

Adviser's name and telephone extension   _____

Date and time you wish to use room

   1st choice _____   **2nd choice** _____

Number of persons expected at meeting   _____

Expected length of meeting   _____

Do you wish to use any of the following? Check appropriate boxes:

Videocassette player ☐   Tape recorder ☐   Movie projector ☐   Slide projector ☐

Signature: _____

Date: _____

1. Why do the directions ask you to use a ball-point pen and to press

hard? __**The application is in duplicate.**_____

2. Why are you asked to print everything except your signature?

Printing is usually easier to read than writing._____

Name _____

Decide in which reference sources you might look for the information requested. Write the name of one or more of the reference sources listed in the box on the line after each item.

> encyclopedia   *Books in Print*   *Contemporary Authors*
> almanac   *Something About the Author*   biographical dictionary
>   *Readers' Guide to Periodical Literature*

1. a list of biographies of Louis Braille that are currently available

Books in Print _____

2. basic information about Louis Braille and the Braille system

encyclopedia, biographical dictionary _____

3. a list of Jean Little's other books

Something About the Author*, *Books in Print*, *Contemporary Authors ___

4. information on the Special Olympics

encyclopedia, *Readers' Guide to Periodical Literature* ___

5. a biography of I. King Jordan, Jr., the first deaf president of Gallaudet University, the only liberal arts college for the deaf in the United States

Books in Print _____

6. up-to-date statistics on disability benefits

almanac _____

7. recent information on civil rights bills concerning people who are disabled

***Readers' Guide to Periodical Literature*, almanac** _____

8. information about William Gibson, who wrote *The Miracle Worker,* a play about Helen Keller and Annie Sullivan

Something About the Author*, *Contemporary Authors ___

• • • THE BRACELET • • •

Name _____

A. Read the following paragraphs. Circle the context clues that helped you determine the meaning of each underlined word. Then write each word on the line next to its meaning.

The huge barrack loomed up in front of our eyes, (one building in row after row of ugly housing.) My family was being evacuated (from our real home) during the threatening early days of World War II.

The United States government feared the presence of (enemy) aliens on its soil, even though most of us were (United States citizens.) We were interned for (several long years,) finally (being allowed to leave) at the end of the war.

1. ___**interned**___ confined or kept from leaving

2. ___**barrack**___ a building where soldiers or other people are housed

3. ___**evacuated**___ removed

4. ___**aliens**___ foreigners

B. Use each of the underlined words in a sentence of your own.
1. **Students' sentences will vary.** _____

_____

2. _____

_____

3. _____

_____

4. _____

_____

THE BRACELET

Name _____

Fill in the story-events chart. **Accept reasonable responses. Possible answers are provided.**

MAJOR EVENT IN STORY	HOW RURI FEELS ABOUT EVENT
Ruri is forced to leave her home.	lonely, empty, abandoned
Laurie Madison gives Ruri a bracelet.	grateful, but sad about leaving Laurie
Ruri's family goes to the Civil Control Station.	scared by soldiers and guns
The family is moved to a stall at a racetrack.	very disappointed
Ruri loses her new bracelet.	heartbroken
Ruri's mother gives her advice.	more hopeful and optimistic

Name _____

Read the passages, and answer the questions.

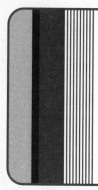

> **M**illy rushed breathlessly into the dining room, slinging her book bag into the corner. "Sorry I'm late," she gasped. Then she noticed that no one was saying anything. Her father sat gripping his silverware, his face a mottled red, his features frozen. Her mother was eating but hardly seemed to be aware of it. Both of Milly's younger sisters were staring into their plates, silent, refusing to meet her eyes.

1. What is this passage mainly about? **Milly's family has been having an argument or some other upsetting confrontation just before she comes into the room.**

2. What details support this main idea? **All the family members are acting strained. No one talks to Milly.**

> **P**eter yawned and rubbed his eyes. He was resting on his arms, which lay across the library computer. Still yawning, he gathered up his books and walked out of the office. He was surrounded by silence, and the darkness surprised him. Only dim hall lights were on. He strolled to the front door and pushed on it; it was locked. He then made his way to the back exit, but it was barred. "Hmm, wonder if I can find a window to open," thought Peter.

3. What is this passage mainly about? **Peter has fallen asleep while working at the library and has been locked in.**

4. What details support this main idea? **He is yawning and has been in a part of the library where people might not be aware of him. The library is dark, and the doors are locked.**

THE BRACELET

Name _____

Imagine you are looking at a book about World War II. Decide which of
the following book parts you would use to find each piece of information.
You may list more than one part for some answers.

| title page | copyright page | contents page | preface |
| appendix | bibliography | glossary | index |

1. descriptions of German war planes and the correct spellings of
   their names
   glossary, index

2. whether the information in the book is arranged chronologically, by
   battle, or by theater (area) of operation
   contents page

3. how up-to-date the book is compared to other books you have read on
   the same subject
   copyright page

4. what sources the author consulted before writing the book
   bibliography, appendix

5. whether there are maps to show the Pacific island battles
   appendix, index

6. information on Generals Eisenhower, MacArthur, and Rommel
   index

7. why the author wrote the book
   preface

8. who published the book
   title page, copyright page

• • • From Life to Poetry • • •

Name _____

A. Read each sentence. Underline the word or group of words that
explains the boldface word.

1. My parents were so impressed with our class's performing arts show
   that their excitement **subsided,** or died down, only after several hours.

2. The classroom had been **partitioned** into several areas, and each group
   performed in its own section.

3. In our area, the drama group performed **impromptu** skits, thought up
   on the spur of the moment.

4. In the poetry corner, some of the recited poems had a strong regular
   rhythm, while others seemed to have no **meter** at all.

5. The budding novelists and short story writers read aloud scenes from
   their **prose** works.

B. Read each question. Write your answer on the line.

1. If the rain subsided, would you put your umbrella up or down?
   down

2. If a room is partitioned, is a wall removed or added?
   added

3. Which of the following is prose, a collection of poems or a news
   magazine? **a news magazine**

4. If a poem has a regular pattern of accented and unaccented syllables,
   does it have meter? **yes**

5. To give an impromptu speech, would you write it out first?
   no

FROM LIFE TO POETRY

Name _____

Begin completing the poetry comment chart on this page. Complete it on another sheet of paper. Your completed chart should follow this pattern and end with Common Reasons for Writing:

Responses will vary. See pages 547D and 560A in the Teacher's Edition for possible answers.

PATTERN FOR CHART

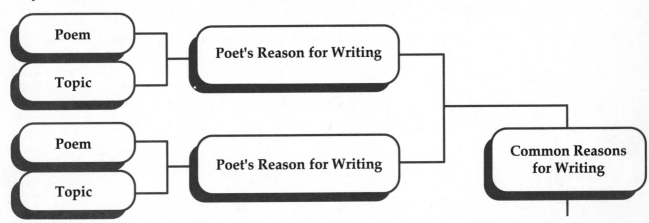

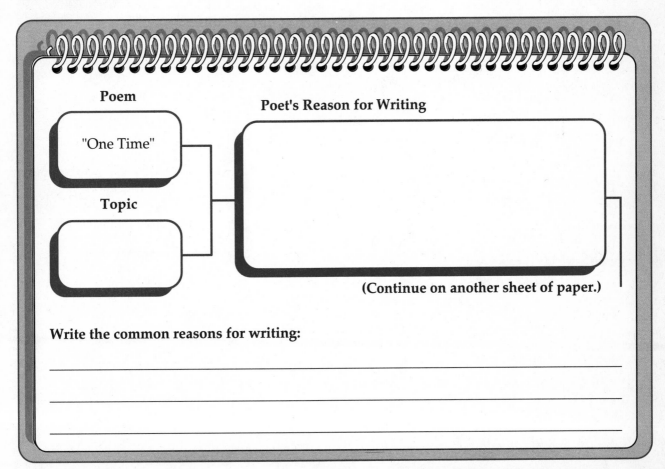

Poem

"One Time"

Topic

Poet's Reason for Writing

(Continue on another sheet of paper.)

Write the common reasons for writing:

_____

_____

_____

FROM LIFE TO POETRY

Name _____

On the lines next to each poem, name the poetic elements that are found in the lines of poetry. Choose your answers from the elements given in the box.

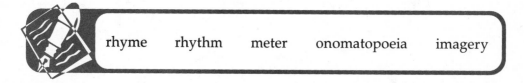

> rhyme   rhythm   meter   onomatopoeia   imagery

1. from **Arithmetic**
Arithmetic is where numbers fly like pigeons in and out of your head.
        Carl Sandburg

rhythm, imagery

2. There was a young farmer of Leeds
Who swallowed six packets of seeds.
It soon came to pass
He was covered with grass,
And he couldn't sit down for the weeds.
        Unknown

rhyme, rhythm, meter

3. Winter Moon
How thin and sharp is the moon tonight!
How thin and sharp and ghostly white
Is the slim curved crook of the moon tonight!
        Langston Hughes

rhythm, rhyme, imagery

4. The lightning flashes!
And slashing through the darkness,
A night-heron's screech.
        Matsuo Bashō

rhythm, imagery,

onomatopoeia

5. from **The Bells**
Keeping time, time, time,
In a sort of runic rhyme,
To the tintinnabulation that so musically wells
From the bells, bells, bells, bells
Bells, bells, bells—
        Edgar Allan Poe

rhyme, rhythm, meter,

onomatopoeia

• • • FROM LIFE TO POETRY • • •

Name _____

Read the paragraphs by three poets. Then write a generalization based on each paragraph.

1. Many people say that they don't like poetry or they don't understand it. But these same people can feel a prickle on their necks or a burning tear in the eye when they see their country's flag waving or hear a moving piece of music. That's what poetry is—emotion—and everyone can feel it.

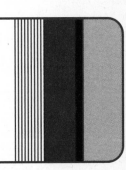

Accept reasonable responses: Everyone can feel and understand the

emotion in poetry.

2. To me, poetry must express the deepest truth of which I am capable. Whether a poem talks about how a tree looks in the sunset or a broken-down car, it means nothing if it is not truthful.

Accept reasonable responses: Poetry must reflect the truth.

3. A poem does not have to rhyme. It may be written about anything: family, the moon, a haystack, an ant. It's the rhythm and the sounds of words that make a poem. A person knows a poem is a poem when he or she feels the rhythm and hears the music in the words.

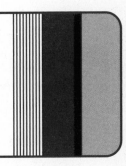

Accept reasonable responses: A combination of rhythm and the sounds of

words makes up a poem.

HBJ material copyrighted under notice appearing earlier in this work.

• • • FROM LIFE TO POETRY • • •

Name _____

Read the two selections, and complete the exercise.

A. I was walking in the hills one day and feeling very alone. Suddenly I saw a field of daffodils. I realized that I wasn't alone, that both the flowers and I were part of nature. How could I feel alone in such a crowd? I sat down to watch the flowers blowing in the wind.

B.   from **I Wandered Lonely as a Cloud**

I wandered lonely as a cloud   Continuous as the stars that shine
That floats on high o'er vales and hills,   And twinkle on the milky way,
When all at once I saw a crowd,   They stretched in never-ending line
A host, of golden daffodils;   Along the margin of a bay:
Beside the lake, beneath the trees,   Ten thousand saw I at a glance,
Fluttering and dancing in the breeze.   Tossing their heads in sprightly dance.
                                                     William Wordsworth

1. Which is a poem? _____ **selection B** _____ Which is a prose
statement? _____ **selection A** _____

2. Which selection describes a solitary walk in the hills? _____ **both** _____

3. Which selection uses modern informal language? _____ **selection A** _____ Which uses
figurative and formal language? _____ **selection B** _____

4. Which selection tells mostly about how the daffodils looked to the writer?
_____ **selection B** _____ Which tells about finding company in
nature? _____ **selection A** _____

5. Which selection best conveys the writer's feelings upon seeing a field of daffodils? Explain
your answer. _____ **Possible answers: Selection A best conveys the change in the**
writer's feelings, since he or she refers to it directly: "I realized that I wasn't
alone." Selection B best conveys the writer's excitement upon seeing the
daffodils, with images that help the reader see and feel the same emotions.

Name _____

A. Complete the story by writing a word from the box on each line.

gaggle	disengaged	slavering	hefted
cache	diminished	wraiths	

Carl __**hefted**__ the last heavy box onto the horse cart and set off for the mountain town a day's ride away. His dog Shadow followed along, as usual preferring to run rather than ride. Carl had taken only a water container, for he knew where there was a __**cache**__ of food halfway between his house and the town. He had hidden it there himself on a previous trip.

The weather was beautiful, windy and sunny. A lovely __**gaggle**__ of geese flew overhead, and quail darted across the roadway like __**wraiths**__ that disappeared before you were sure they were there.

Toward noon the wind __**diminished**__ somewhat, and Carl realized how hot the sun was without the cooling breeze. He looked back to see Shadow __**slavering**__ and panting. "Come on, silly one, get in the cart," Carl clucked to the dog. "The food supply is just around the bend, and I'll pour you some water, too."

Carl soon drove into a meadow, and Shadow watched from the cart seat as Carl __**disengaged**__ the horses from their harnesses to let them graze. Soon all of them—boy, horses, and dog—were eating contentedly.

B. Choose four of the vocabulary words. On a separate sheet of paper, use each in a sentence of your own.
Sentences will vary.

• • • DOGSONG • • •

Name _____

Fill in the cause and effect chain.

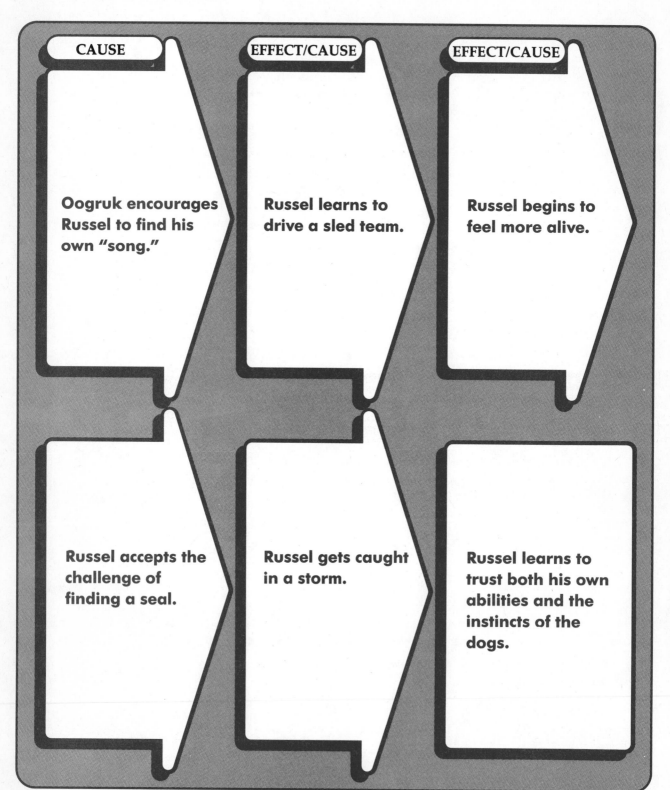

CAUSE

Oogruk encourages Russel to find his own "song."

EFFECT/CAUSE

Russel learns to drive a sled team.

EFFECT/CAUSE

Russel begins to feel more alive.

Russel accepts the challenge of finding a seal.

Russel gets caught in a storm.

Russel learns to trust both his own abilities and the instincts of the dogs.

• • • DOGSONG • • •

Name _____

Choose the correct word to complete each analogy, and write it on the line.

1. *Note* is to *tune* as *word* is to _**poem**_____.
   (vowel, school, poem, mouth)

2. *Snow* is to *solid* as *water* is to _**liquid**_____.
   (ice, liquid, boil, melt)

3. *Ptarmigan* is to *bird* as *seal* is to _**mammal**_____.
   (fish, blubber, fur, mammal)

4. *Lamp* is to *light* as *stove* is to _**heat**_____.
   (coal, heat, oven, gas)

5. *Human* is to *hair* as *fish* is to _**scales**_____.
   (fins, gills, scales, swim)

6. *Hood* is to *head* as *mitten* is to _**hand**_____.
   (wool, warm, knitted, hand)

7. *Harpoon* is to *weapon* as *sled* is to _**vehicle**_____.
   (vehicle, wood, runners, dogs)

8. *Oil* is to *fuel* as *meat* is to _**food**_____.
   (seal, harpoon, food, hungry)

9. *Harness* is to *leather* as *sled* is to _**wood**_____.
   (drag, wood, ice, speed)

10. *Teeth* is to *bite* as *claws* is to _**scratch**_____.
    (cat, sharp, scratch, paws)

• • • DOGSONG • • •

Name _____

Read each sentence from the story, and notice the underlined referents. Then answer each question with a single word or a group of words.

"Oogruk explained how the people of the village once had songs but lost them when they abandoned traditional ways."

1. To what does them refer? _____ **songs** _____

2. To what does they refer? _____ **people** _____

"It was the old kind of sled . . ."

3. To what does It refer? _____ **sled** _____

"(Russel) knew when he put his feet to the sled and took the handlebar in his hands that they would run, and he did not know how he knew this but only that it was so."

4. To what do this and it refer? _____ **that they would run** _____

"The feeling, (Russel) thought, the feeling is that the sled is alive; that I am alive and the sled is alive and the snow is alive and the ice is alive and we are all part of the same life."

5. To what does I refer? _____ **Russel** _____

6. To what does we refer? _____ **Russel, the sled, the snow, and the ice** _____

"Oogruk wanted oil for the lamp and he wanted some seal meat and fat to eat and he said these things in such a way that Russel felt it would be good to find a seal to take with the harpoon."

7. To what does he refer? _____ **Oogruk** _____

8. To what does these things refer? _____ **that Oogruk wanted oil, seal meat, and fat** _____

_____

Name _____

Read the sentences. Underline the correct meaning for the boldface word
in each sentence.

1. As Regina raised the tent flap, she heard her mutt Maggie **emit** a
low growl.

    muffle   pretend   <u>give off</u>   bark

2. Regina was **gratified** that Maggie had smelled the intruder, but she
knew that it was only a harmless raccoon.

    disgusted   confused   confident   <u>pleased</u>

3. Maggie was curled into the sleeping bag, her **brindle** coat blending
with the tan interior of the bag.

    black   <u>tawny</u>   red   white

4. Regina stepped from the tent but suddenly found herself **floundering**
and almost falling in several inches of water.

    swimming   wading   walking   <u>struggling</u>

5. As she moved her tent to higher ground, Regina remembered the
resounding thunder that had wakened her during the night.

    distant   quiet   <u>loud</u>   long-lasting

6. "Fine," she thought, "this trip we get caught in a flood, while last time
we almost **plummeted** off a glacier into a crevasse. I'd better improve
my camping skills."

    <u>plunged</u>   sank   crawled   slid

Name _____

Complete the main idea chart. **Accept reasonable responses. Examples are provided.**

NAME OF DOG	WHAT THE DOG DID	THE LESSON GARY PAULSEN LEARNED
Cookie	**deliberately led team into gully; held 18-hour "sit-down strike"**	**Humans should respect and trust the dogs' instincts or suffer serious consequences.**
Storm	**hid objects, such as Paulsen's hat** **growled at the stove**	**Dogs have a sense of humor; they play practical jokes.** **Dogs can express objections.**

Name _____

Read the passage about painting a room, and answer the questions.

HOW TO PAINT YOUR BEDROOM

First, collect your equipment. This should include paint, stirring sticks, water, brushes and rollers, drop cloths, plastic sheeting, newspapers, a bucket for cleaning brushes, and a stepladder.

Second, prepare the area to be painted. Move all the small items and pieces of furniture out of your room. Then shove all the large furniture away from the walls and cover it with drop cloths. Also put plastic sheeting and newspapers around the borders of the room to catch paint drippings.

When you are ready to go to work, open the paint can and stir the paint to mix thoroughly. Paint the ceiling first to avoid having to repaint the walls. After you have finished painting the entire room, put the brushes and rollers into a bucket of water to soak. Then, pick up all the protective coverings.

Finally, move all the furniture back into place. You now have a new room.

1. What should you do before you begin any of the steps?
Read the directions through twice.
_____

_____

2. If you were to divide this task into four basic steps, what would they be called?
1. Collecting the equipment
_____
2. Preparing the area to be painted
_____
3. Painting
_____
4. Cleaning up the room and arranging the furniture
_____

3. List at least three signal words that tell you about following directions.
Students may choose from *first, second, then, when, after,* and *finally*.
_____

_____

Name _____

Read the passages, and complete the exercises.

The two female kittens were inseparable from birth. When they were four, Tarlin died of a virus. Molly seemed to mourn for her sister. She walked around meowing pitifully for days. She looked into closets and cupboards. She peered into my face as if she could read the answer there. She sat in the window as still as a statue. Molly only became her old self again when we took in a stray cat from the neighborhood.

1. Circle the letter next to the sentence that best states the main idea of the passage.
   a. Tarlin died of a virus.
   (b.) Molly seemed to mourn for her sister.
   c. The two female kittens were inseparable from birth.

2. Cite three details from the passage to support your choice.
   The kittens were inseparable from birth. Molly walked around meowing pitifully after Tarlin died. She looked for her sister. She sat quietly in a window. She perked up when a new cat appeared.

One day I hid my dog Jack's food bowl. When he found it, he looked at me with a look of such reproach that I felt sheepish. He refused to eat anything that day or the next. He also left any room I entered, no matter how comfortable he had been when I walked in. It took him a long time to forgive me.

3. Circle the letter next to the sentence that best states the main idea of the passage.
   a. Jack loses his appetite easily.
   b. Jack never forgives anything.
   (c.) Jack does not like to be tricked.

4. Cite three details from the passage to support your choice.
   Jack gave the writer a reproachful look when he found his bowl. He refused to eat for two days. He left any room the writer entered.

Name _____

Read the following selection, and complete the exercises.

When the Wheatons went on vacation, they asked their neighbor, Anne, to walk and feed their dog, Major. The first day they were gone, Major got away from Anne and disappeared. Anne searched and searched and then, returning home, she waited anxiously for the Wheatons to call.

The Wheaton boys, Leroy and Mac, were both upset when they learned of Major's disappearance. They asked where Anne had looked. "Everywhere," she replied. "Did you get as far as the entrance to the highway?" asked Leroy. "N-o-o-o," she answered, puzzled.

"We play a tracking game with Major," said Leroy, breathlessly. "One of us distracts him while the other goes off somewhere and hides, sometimes as far away as three miles. Then Major tracks our smell and finds us. If he began tracking the family car, he could probably follow us only as far as the highway entrance before our smell would be lost in the confusion of all the traffic. Please, Anne, would you look there? We'll call back in an hour."

Without much hope, Anne drove to the highway ramp. There was Major lying in the grass on the hill, his nose pointed in the direction they had driven. "C'mon, boy. I know you miss them, but they'll be home soon," said Anne as she led him to the car.

1. Write a brief summary of the selection on another sheet of paper.
Students' wording will vary but should include only the main ideas.

2. Did you state in your summary that Anne was taking care of Major?

Why or why not? ___**yes, because it is a main idea**_____

3. Did you include the tracking-game distance of three miles? Why or why not?
no, because it is only a detail

4. Did you include the relationship between the game and finding Major?
Why or why not?
yes, because it is a main idea

SKILLS AND STRATEGIES INDEX

DECODING

Structural Analysis 43–44, 50, 94, 108, 129
    Combining forms 129
    Greek and Latin roots 94, 129
    Prefixes 43–44, 50, 94, 108, 129
    Suffixes 43–44, 50, 94, 108

VOCABULARY

Analogies 60, 151
Antonyms 60
Connotation and denotation 54, 82, 132
Content area vocabulary 14
Context clues 39, 43–44, 50, 112, 121, 133
Homophones and homographs 72
Key words 1, 6, 12, 18, 24, 30, 36, 41, 48, 52, 58, 63, 70, 76, 80, 86, 91, 95, 100, 104, 110, 114, 118, 124, 130, 136, 140, 144, 149, 153
Multiple-meaning words 102, 112, 121, 133
Vocabulary strategies 43–44

COMPREHENSION

Active reading strategies 4–5, 46–47
Analyzing important details 10–11
Author's purpose and viewpoint 55, 84, 89, 135
Cause and effect 15, 29, 34
Comparing and contrasting 74–75, 103, 106, 134
Drawing conclusions 8, 22, 28
Fact and opinion 66–67, 84, 89, 135
Main idea and details 83, 142, 156
Making generalizations 40, 57, 62, 147
Making inferences 32–33
Making judgments 78–79, 103, 106, 134, 148
Making predictions 16, 22, 28
Paraphrasing 61, 85
Reading fiction 46–47
Reading nonfiction 68–69
Referents 65, 152
Sequence 9, 29, 34
Sequence/cause-effect 29, 34
Summarizing 51, 57, 62, 157
Summarizing/generalizing 57, 62
Summarizing the Literature 2, 7, 13, 19, 25, 31, 37, 42, 49, 53, 59, 64, 71, 77, 81, 87, 92, 96, 101, 105, 111, 115, 119, 125, 131, 137, 141, 145, 150, 154
Synthesizing information 20–21

LITERARY APPRECIATION

Conflict 45
Figurative language 93, 99, 107
Imagery 146
Literary forms 73
Meter 146
Narrative elements
    Character 3, 26–27
    Mood and tone 3, 26–27, 35
    Plot 3, 45
    Setting 3, 35
    Theme 3, 56
Onomatopoeia 146
Poetry 146
Point of view 88
Rhythm and rhyme 146

STUDY SKILLS

Advertisements 120
Book parts 78, 109, 143
Content area vocabulary 14
Directions 116, 138, 155
Forms and applications 138
Graphic aids 98, 117, 127
    Diagrams 127
    Graphs 117
    Maps 98
Index 109
Library skills 79, 113
Reference sources 17, 23, 54, 90, 139
Study strategies 122–123
Synthesizing information 20–21
Test-taking strategies 128
Thesaurus 54

LANGUAGE

Abbreviations 126
Acronyms 126
Advertisements/slanted language 120
Slanted writing 82, 120
Spanish words/pronunciation 38
Word origins 97